THE

Eyes

HAVE IT

THE *Eyes* HAVE IT

As Told By

JEANNE BYRNS

In Writing and Orally
To

SONYA UTTERBACK CIRKS

Order this book online at www.trafford.com
or email orders@trafford.com

Most Trafford titles are also available at major online book retailers.

Printed in the United States of America.

ISBN: 978-1-4269-8167-8 (sc)
ISBN: 978-1-4269-8168-5 (hc)
ISBN: 978-1-4269-8169-2 (e)

Library of Congress Control Number: 2011912827

Trafford rev. 07/29/2011

www.trafford.com

North America & International
toll-free: 1 888 232 4444 (USA & Canada)
phone: 250 383 6864 ♦ fax: 812 355 4082

CONTENTS

PREFACE

By David L. Taunton, PhD

The story of Jeanne Byrns's life is a heart-rending, true account of how a little girl, Jeanne, raised in the Deep South, suffered physical and emotional abuse and neglect, physically and emotionally throughout her childhood. Impoverished and unwanted by either parent, Jeanne's home life was a nightmare from which there appeared to be no escape.

Having dealt intimately for many years with hundreds of victims of child abuse, reading Jeanne's story served as a painful reminder of the ongoing suffering of thousands of children across our nation as they struggle to survive.

What has happened to this once great nation, which from its very roots has honored the family unit and cherished its children as its greatest asset? Have we become so caught up in our ever-increasing fast-paced lifestyle that we no longer have time for our children?

In my duel role as a longtime judge and the cofounder of the Taunton Family Children's Home, which has taken in hundreds of "little Jeannes" over the past two decades, my heart cries out for our country to wake up to the horrifying plight of far too many of its children.

Not only will this book help increase awareness of abused and neglected children, but it will also serve as an inspiration and source of hope for those who have suffered lives similar to Jeanne's, for hers is a story of eventual triumph.

Whether or not you have been a victim of child abuse, your life will be deeply impacted by Jeanne's story, skillfully written by author Sonya Cirks and Jeanne Byrns.

FOREWORD

You are about to enter the mind of an abused child, a child whose world is one of darkness with little light and is composed of feelings of intense fear, helplessness, hopelessness, loneliness, isolation, and death. Hers is a world in which fear is a natural state of being ... a way of life, where a child had to become an "instant learner" to be safe and to become accomplished at fading into the background to become "camouflaged," for "if you were invisible you were safe." This child didn't realize that beatings and abuse weren't a way of life for every child. This was a world shaped and formed by what the adults in her life said and did. As Jeanne once said to me, "All a child knows is what adults say." After reading Jeanne's story, one's understanding of her fear-filled world becomes painfully clear. It is our hope that your awareness will increase as well. If you are a parent, may you become more aware of the impact that your words and actions have on your children and the people who are important to you. The old saying "Sticks and stones may break my bones but words will never hurt me" is as far from the truth as one can ever get! In Jeanne's words, "Beatings with words were as lethal as razor straps. Remarks were like invisible stones and unseen knives pounding and lacerating the tenderest place—my sense of self." You, as a parent, are the creator and the interpreter of your child's world. *Never, never, never* forget it!

For those of you who have traveled the painful road of abuse, it is hoped that it will become clear to you as well that you can find hope and healing, as Jeanne has on her journey from victim to victory.

Child abuse and neglect is a national problem that has increased to epidemic proportions in the United States. More than 2.5 million cases of child abuse are reported in the United States annually, and it is estimated that for every reported case three go unreported. Hundreds of children die physically each year as a result of abuse, but even more die emotionally.

Jeanne's story is one of physical, emotional, and sexual abuse as well as neglect in all of its possible forms. However, despite her victimization on all levels it is her experience of emotional abuse that has left the deepest and most lasting scars.

Emotional abuse does not leave physical injuries, and because of the lack of a legal operational definition and a true standard of severity it is the least studied, least reported, and consequently the least prosecuted form of child abuse. In many cases, it is the least recognized as abuse by the perpetrator! In my thirty years of practice I find it to be the most prevalent form of abuse I have seen and the most lethal. Emotional abuse leaves deep scars on a child's emotional development, self-concept, and sense of self-worth. It can be the cruelest and most destructive of all types of abuse, because it destroys the child "from the inside out." Children who are constantly shamed, verbally assaulted, humiliated, terrorized, and rejected suffer as much if not more than if they had been physically assaulted. Physical wounds heal, but the emotional scarring lasts forever. Indeed, emotional abuse is the most difficult form of abuse to identify and stop because of the lack of physical evidence, but the emotional evidence is undeniable. Children who suffer such abuse often grow into adults who still see themselves through the eyes of the abuser.

They carry a sense of inadequacy and worthlessness that permeates every level of their life, their relationships, and their work. Generally, emotional abuse includes a variety of tactics:

- Rejecting and criticizing—letting the child know in a variety of ways that he/she is unwanted, stupid, worthless, and a burden
- Ignoring—showing the child no interest, no affection, no nurturing
- Terrorizing—singling out the child to criticize, punish, ridicule, or threaten with mutilation, abandonment, or death
- Isolation—preventing the child from having normal activities; cutting them off from peers and giving them responsibilities far beyond their age, such as caring for an infant sibling. This leaves them feeling isolated, alone, and in constant fear that they may do something wrong.

- Corrupting—engaging and encouraging the child in deviant behavior

You will see and hear all of these forms of emotional abuse, except corruption, in Jeanne's story.

Emotional abuse leaves hidden scars that can manifest themselves in numerous ways—insecurity, poor self-esteem, destructive behavior, angry acting out, withdrawal, poor development of basic skills, substance abuse, suicide, and difficulty bonding emotionally to another person, although sometimes individuals who have been emotionally abused may become overly fearful, dependent, and clinging. Jeanne's determination, perseverance, and strong faith continue to help her in overcoming the issues in her life, and as a result she has become both a successful medical professional as well as an accomplished artist and sculptor.

Many of you in reading this book will be moved to tears by the pain and the horror of a little girl struggling to survive. Others may find that it awakens unresolved issues and painful memories. Jeanne opens up her life to you and deals honestly with the raw hurts and emotion. Pain becomes her greatest teacher, as it does for all of us. It seems that God uses the most difficult circumstances in our lives to teach us the most important lessons.

In my many years as a therapist dealing with abuse and other types of trauma, I often hear the question "Why would a loving God allow such suffering?" One might ask the same for Jeanne. After seeing many people through their dark nights, an answer seems to be one of personal and spiritual growth as well as responsibility for ourselves and others. It is through traumatic life situations and happenings that God gets our attention! We realize that something is wrong and that something needs to be done to change either ourselves or the world. Traumatic situations also cause us to rethink our priorities as well as our relationship with God. "My strength is made perfect in weakness" (2 Cor. 12:9).

When there is nowhere else to go we turn inward and decide what is really most important. Trauma such as abuse also dramatically forces us to deal with the deeper issues of life. It shapes us. Paul wrote: "Tribulation produces perseverance, perseverance produces character, and character produces hope" (Rom. 5:3–5). It is also by facing our trauma and fear that we grow stronger and gain wisdom and maturity. Finally, pain and suffering have a special ability to show us how much we need each other. Tragedies such as child abuse and neglect place the responsibility on all of us as God's children to be there for each other as well as to work together to alleviate such devastating problems.

Indeed, God can use the most difficult circumstances in our lives to teach us individually as well as in a society the most important lesson: there is strength and healing in our love for one another.

Jeanne's story is a testimony to the triumph of the human spirit over the dark devastation of child abuse. The dark, lonely, frightening, and pain-filled world of uncaring and hurtful adults surrounded her, and yet she was "protected." Jeanne speaks of an awareness of being saved from disaster too many times not to believe the "presence of the Divine" in her life. For Jeanne the pain and trauma she endured both awakened and deepened her faith. It strengthened her character and resolve, allowing her to overcome her fears and scars and move forward. Further, the "sandpaper" of her trauma helped form a deeply loving, compassionate, and creative person who, in her words, "would never have gotten to 'the finish'" if she hadn't gone through all the things she did, just like the butterfly struggling to be free of its cocoon (bondage). Because of the long struggle for freedom, its wings become strong enough to fly. It is through our struggles that we gain strength, compassion, wisdom, understanding, and vision. It is one's hope that Jeanne's story will bring awareness, understanding, and the potential for change both on a personal level as well on the level of social responsibility, for "we are our brother's keeper." Perhaps God in his infinite wisdom has brought Jeanne to this time and place in her life that she might share her story to bring awareness, understanding, hope, and light to others. In Viktor Frankl's words, "What is to give light must endure burning."

Joan L. Kogelschatz, PhD
Nationally certified psychologist
Board-certified traumatologist
Past president, State of Alabama Child Abuse and Neglect Advisory Board

Joan Kogelschatz, PhD
Nationally certified psychologist
Board-certified traumatologist
Past president, State of Alabama Child Abuse and Neglect Advisory
Board

Dr. Kogelschatz is a psychotherapist who has been in private practice in Dothan, Alabama, for twenty-six years. Prior to coming to Dothan she was on staff in the department of psychiatry at the University of Florida Medical Center for six and a half years.

She has served as a consultant in child and adolescent psychiatry to St. Vincent's Hospital and Duvall Medical Center in Jacksonville, Florida, and is a member of the American Association of Psychiatric Services for Children and the National Council on Family Relations and is a clinical member of the American Association of Marriage and Family Therapists.

In 1980 Dr. Kogelschatz was appointed by former Alabama governor Fob James to the Alabama Law Enforcement Planning Agency Advisory Board, a board that is involved in the planning and funding of juvenile delinquent and adult criminal evaluation centers. She has held offices on the Dothan Child Abuse Prevention Board, the Alabama Society of Crippled Children and Adults Board, and the Girls Club of Dothan Board and has been on the advisory boards of the Adam Group, an organization for providing therapeutic treatment for the wife abuser, and the "Compassionate Friends," an organization to assist parents who have lost a child through death.

From 1984 to 1986 Dr. Kogelschatz was president of the Second Congressional District Council on Child Abuse and Neglect. She was instrumental in establishing a thirteen-county council to assist in the development and funding of child-abuse prevention programs. In 1985 she was selected to be on the advisory committee of the State of Alabama Child Abuse and Neglect Prevention Board. She was elected president of that state advisory board in 1985 and was reelected as president from 1985 to 1990.

Dr. Kogelschatz has been selected by the Dothan Chamber of Commerce for Leadership Dothan and was selected to be listed in *Who's Who of American Women, Who's Who of the South and Southwest, Who's*

Who among Human Service Professionals, Distinguished Leaders in Health Care, Notable American Women, the *World's Who's Who of Women,* and the *International Who's Who of Professional and Business Women.* She was selected as "Woman of the Year" for 1983 by the National Federation of Business and Professional Women and in 1998 was selected as "Model Woman of the Year" by the Girls Clubs of Dothan. In 1999–2000 she was selected for *Who's Who in Medicine and Healthcare* and was included in *Who's Who of American Women, 2000–2001.*

Prologue

SURVIVOR

He was the largest yet. She had never attempted one that big. Friends said it had the most realistic facial expression of any of her sculptures. She herself was thrilled with it; you could tell.

"I'm calling it 'Exile from Eden,'" she declared.

His face was twisted in agony. One arm was flung out to his right, fingers slightly bent as if cupping a ball, clutching the air in a mute "No!" The other arm was bent, fist closed, across his forehead, palm outward. His face expressed indelible torment.

"Jeanne, that sculpture won't fit in our kiln," her teacher advised. Regretfully, she cut Adam's out-flung arm off at the bicep. Then came the period of patience every sculptor knows: waiting for it to dry thoroughly.

Weeks later it was put into the kiln, and the next day Jeanne rushed to school to see how he came out. "As I peered into the cooled-down kiln, I was staggered," she groaned. "His tormented face was intact, but everything else was flayed, cracked, or deformed. Several holes pierced his side and back. Below his chest much of his skin looked as if a whip had simply peeled off layer after layer of flesh. Adam was ruined.

"I took him home and sat him on the living room floor, where he stayed for weeks as I passed repeatedly by and let his broken body sink its jagged edges into my soul. I mulled him over and over in my mind each passing time. Finally, in a fit of irony, I flung bandages about his body."

She left the bandaged Adam there for weeks more.

"Then one day I began again to take a hard look at him. This is no longer Adam, 'Exile from Eden.' This has become something else by virtue of all it has endured. I think now I'm going to call it 'The High Price of Freedom.' Around him I will put a miniature graveyard, a picture of the Vietnam Wall, and a telegram with the words 'We regret to inform you.' Also there will be a table set for three, with Mother and Father each sitting there. The third chair will be empty. Nearby I'll put a book of rationing stamps from WWII and a packet of letters with an APO address, tied in a yellow ribbon. Elsewhere on the base I'll have a bombed-out school. Near it there will be some black people lying face down beside a burning church."

The more she talked, the more her friend became excited at the originality of the concept.

"I suddenly realized that this is Jeanne!" her friend exclaimed. "This is what she has done all her life, with her life. When it was shattered, when everything seemed destroyed or ripped beyond repair, she looked in a different direction and found a new concept to begin working on. This is how she survived when so many were destroyed.

"Now I realize," she mused, "that all of us are both sculptor and sculpture. Our life is the clay. We can go through fires and destruction, and perhaps the devastation will leave only a shattered shell of our former selves, but even though we are in pieces, we are still all there and it is up to us to salvage the pieces, to reshape and remodel them. What comes out may be more powerful, more inspiring, more rewarding than the original."

Jeanne Byrns's sculptures call us all to learn the art of survival sculpture in the shadowed places of our souls. By surviving herself, by conquering the shadows, she has shown that it can be done. It is possible to survive and find the sunshine. Carry on!

A PARABLE

A parable is told of a farmer who owned an old mule.

One day the mule fell into the farmer's well. The farmer heard the mule braying. After carefully assessing the situation, the farmer sympathized with the mule but decided that neither the mule nor the well was worth the trouble of saving. Instead he called his neighbors together and enlisted them to help haul dirt to bury the old mule in the well and put him out of his misery.

Initially the old mule was hysterical. But as the farmer and his neighbors continued shoveling and as the dirt hit his back ... a thought struck him. It suddenly dawned on him that every time a shovel load of dirt landed on his back, *he should shake it off and step up!* This he did, blow after blow.

It wasn't long before the old mule, battered and exhausted, stepped triumphantly over the wall of the well! What seemed like that which would bury him actually blessed him ... all because of the manner in which he handled his adversity.

*That's life! If we face our problems and respond to them positively and refuse to give in to panic, bitterness, or self-pity, the adversities that come along to bury us usually have within them the potential to benefit and bless us! Remember that forgiveness, faith, prayer, praise, and hope are all excellent ways to "*shake it off and step up*" out of the wells of despair in which we sometimes find ourselves.*

Chapter One

__WALMART__

The day was sun-curled: a Floridian's summer delight. To turn from the sun into an air-conditioned building like the local Walmart made me feel iced all over, washed with cool. It was a "just right" day. Suddenly I stopped, my feet glued to the floor. My hands became blocks of wood, and my heart started hammering in fear.

In the entryway among the clutter of food machines and weekly specials a bench held two unkempt, long-haired men with a little girl sitting between them. She looked about eight or ten. The men were obviously friends or perhaps even brothers. The little girl wore drab clothes no child would have taken joy in. She had a neglected, unkempt air. Her hair was straight and stringy, her clothes colorless and wrinkled. As I entered the store, the larger man was trying to force her head down into his lap. She resisted. The thinner, second man laughed when the beefy man slammed her head back down into his coveralls. "I tol' ya to keep yoah head down, girl!" he threatened as he pushed it back onto his knees. After a moment she lifted her head the smallest bit and looked straight at me. It was a look that halted me in mid-step and shot deeply into my heart.

Her eyes pled, begging me to help. They were the eyes of a trapped animal looking for escape. But there was no escape for her and, oh God!—I knew she was helpless and I was too. Waves of grief, rage, and frustration washed over me. She dared to raise her head a little more when our eyes locked. Brutally, he pushed it back down into his lap. The second man gave a gravelly laugh. My heart broke for the girl. It broke for me. It broke for all the wounded children of the world, abused and torn, and the memories of all such adults.

I wanted to snatch her up and pull her to safety, but I knew there was nothing I could do. What could I say? There was nothing specific I could put my finger on as a charge, and the only evidence I had was her eyes. Could I say, "Look at her eyes. Can't you tell she is abused?" How could I explain that to a policeman or a store manager? Could I march up to the men and tell them to stop or I would report them? They would only laugh at me or be enraged with the girl. Anything I might say to the men themselves would only make it worse for her. There was no way to intervene. Her helplessness—and mine—broke open the scabs of memory. Do you know what it's like to be unable to ask for rescue or help; to be helpless to act, unable to rescue, incapable of helping? It was an unknown child on that Walmart bench, but it was me too. I knew how she felt; I had been there myself, and to this day, I grieve for her and for my inability to help her.

Her eyes haunt me still. Once I lived behind eyes like that. My memory stretches back like a piece of overused elastic. Like her eyes, it haunts me. The pain has followed me down through the years, stalking my thoughts and affecting my life in a multitude of ways.

I never thought I would be telling my story, yet I have come to realize that I have been writing it on my heart and in my head for decades. A living tableau of pain, it is my journal of hell. If you dare descend to it with me I am now ready to tell you what hell is like in the eyes of one who has walked its walk. Perhaps your knowing will make a difference to some future child or aged person, or even to yourself.

An aged person who is dependent on help is fearful of retaliation if she complains. It isn't necessary to beat her; lack of love is enough. Remember that there is covert abuse as well as overt abuse. There is even inadvertent abuse, when we get so snarled in self that we become unable to see that our lack of love is strangling another's soul. In today's world there are many inadvertent abusers.

Studies done in WWII show that institutionalized orphans, deprived of touch, were unable to develop normally. Sometimes they simply turned their faces to the wall and died. Others became retarded for lack of stimuli. Some of today's Russian and Romanian orphans have become autistic or catatonic from sensory neglect. *Lack of love kills.*

Abuse comes in many forms, some more violent than others but each deadly in its own way. Abuse kills, whether it is overt, inadvertent, or covert. But before it kills, it stifles the soul, which is why some elderly are afraid to complain and why abused children live in ongoing "kitchens of hell." Something painful is always being cooked up for them.

Like the time I was certain I was going to die. The reason I was so sure was because my parents told me so. Little children believe their parents; it is all they know. Their parents are their world, the rock of their existence. Do you know what it's like as a child to be sure of death and to know that your dying doesn't matter to one single person on earth? That is not teasing for the child. If it scars the memory, it is abuse.

Abused people of any age are often afraid to speak. Their eyes are all that speak for them. Look at the eyes. Look into the eyes. Do they contain knowledge of death like mine did, the time I was eight and thought I would be dead in a few hours? Look into the eyes. Look … and see. The eyes tell the story.

Chapter Two

DADDY AND MOTHER

My grandparents were good, hardworking, respectable people. My mother and aunts were well raised. When she was eighteen and just out of high school, my mother met my father, who was a worldly, handsome twenty-five-year-old army man. It wasn't very long before they decided to marry. My grandparents objected in vain to such a youthful and impetuous marriage, but World War II was on and life was short. Mother wouldn't listen.

From the beginning my mother and father's relationship was volatile. He was an extremely jealous man, even though he was very handsome and very intelligent. My mother was a beautiful woman. Maybe she did enjoy all the looks she received from the young officers, as Daddy accused. Who knows? But who would be jealous of looks?

I was the firstborn; Joy followed twelve months later. Joy had our mother's blue eyes and looked like a baby doll. In fact, she wore Aunt BeBe's doll clothes when we had the picture taken for our family portrait.

Sometime after my birth the army moved us to Louisiana. The barracks we lived in had two stories. Mother was pregnant with Joy then, and climbing two stories was difficult for her. She would have to go down to take me out to play and stay with me—not much fun for a busy pregnant woman who had things to do upstairs. She solved that problem very easily. She hitched me to a clothesline so I was out of her hair and could run from one end of the line to the other in my old metal stroller. Then she could just look out the window and see how I was doing. Even after little Joy was born, my mother continued to tie my stroller to the clothesline to get me out of her hair.

She told me about it the summer I lived with her, and even though I don't remember it, I still cringe at the idea of being tied to a clothesline at the age of one and left for hours, untended, wet, and often hungry, no doubt. Anything could have happened to me. Should any child ever be leashed and left alone? That story is something I've never forgotten, although why that should bother me in the light of later events is a mystery. Funny how some things just hang around in your head for no good reason and you can't seem to scrape them away. I always see the picture of a helpless, tethered animal at the beck and control of its master when I think of that story of Mother's. I guess it wasn't only the lack of humaneness that bothers me; it was also the utter lack of control I had then or for years to come to change anything in my life; any of my circumstances. So many of us are trapped simply because we are children. We may have no control over our own lives right now, but we can control our ultimate destinies (eventually, if not immediately).

Sometimes at night my father drank. When he drank he always got very jealous. Once he chased my mother around the barracks kitchen with a butcher knife because he said she'd flirted with some guys on the train. He was the one who told us that. I was a teenager when I first heard the story. He used to laugh as he told it. Actually, she'd had two little girls on her lap according to what she told me later. The men had given up their seats and helped her with us. Daddy surmised that she egged guys on.

Who knows? Maybe she did. Perhaps a young, exceptionally pretty woman tied down by marriage and two children thought there was nothing wrong with a little flirting to boost one's morale. If she never went beyond that, where was the harm? But she may not even have done that. It depends on who you believed. Through the years, as we bounced back and forth between parents we got different versions of their marriage. I hated that controlling, jealous streak in Daddy. It was totally irrational. Later, when I understood, I also abhorred my mother's self-absorption. It was totally repugnant and deleterious.

When she got pregnant with Ray, Daddy was a master sergeant at Bakers and Cooks School in Louisiana. As a master sergeant, Daddy had full hospital privileges and could afford the best of care. Instead, he sent Mother to her parent's farm where she had no doctor, no pain killers, and no anesthesia. He sent her to my grandparents because he "didn't want her flirting with some army doctor"! He said that if home birth had been good enough for him, it was good enough for their baby too. She begged to have a doctor, but he was adamant. He chose instead to endanger this nine-months-pregnant woman by sending her back home because he thought she'd flirt with the doctors while she gave birth!

After three days of labor, the baby, which weighed over ten pounds, literally had to be pulled out of her. It nearly cost her her life. She got gangrene from the placenta, which the rural midwife neglected to take out completely, and nearly died. It was an experience straight out of hell, and because of it she was terrified of having another child.

I believe she always associated Ray with the pain of that birth. She never had much to do with Baby Ray; she never held him or played with him. She didn't even like the smell of baby powder. He was clean and fed, but there was no nurturing for him. Little Ray had her blue eyes and was a chubby, undemanding baby boy. He was cute and sweet, but not to her, and there was no bonding between them.

On Christmas Eve the year I was four, we all—Daddy too—went to church. It was a special Christmas Eve service, and Joy and I each had something under the church tree. There were lots of special wrapped packages there—one for each child. Joy and I were so excited! During the service, Baby Ray wet on Mother's lap. Suddenly, she jerked upright as the warmth spread to her lap. She pushed him away from her, half rose, and literally dropped him to the floor in anger and disgust, staring at the soiled spot on her new blue suit. Ray sat on the floor sobbing and screaming. I remember the voice of a strange lady saying to her, "Why Edna, how could you?" After the strange lady said that, Daddy picked Ray up and we left. Joy and I never got our gifts. Even though it didn't involve me, it was another incident I never forgot because it showed such a lack of maternal love. We were to learn a lot more about that lack when our stepmother Jean came into our lives. But that all was still in our future. Perhaps one of God's kindnesses to us is that we can't see into the future.

I believe of the three of us Ray is the one most harmed by all we went through. Unable to trust, unloved, his life is now a shambles. I remember him as a chubby little two-year-old in corduroy overalls, riding the stick horse that Grandma Love made him. After we moved from their farm, he always kept his hands in his pockets so he wouldn't get them slapped. He was a quick learner.

Nine months after Ray's birth my mother was pregnant again. She cried and screamed and begged my father, saying that she couldn't go through that again, that she must go to a hospital, but he repeated his "homebirth" philosophy. A few days later, when he went to work at the base, she left us with a neighbor and went to a back-street Louisiana abortionist. This was before *Rowe v. Wade*. When Daddy found out he said she'd killed his baby and he was going to kill her. There was never any forgiveness or understanding in him. The next day he filed for divorce.

Just like that the marriage was over. No question of working it out, seeking counseling, or just listening, trying to see the other side. It was just over. That says a lot about my father, but of course I was too young to understand at the time. I only knew that "divorce" had to be one of the ugliest words in any language. Sometime after the divorce, Mother returned alone to Florida.

Around that time Daddy had married a woman named Bess, who married him, we learned later, only to have a little boy. We lived with them because that is how my mother wanted it, I guess. She didn't want to be bothered with us.

As a result of his "high intelligence and leadership qualities," Daddy was given the opportunity to go to officers candidate school. They called it Operation Bootstrap. One morning after a few months of OCS, while Daddy was training at the army base, Bess disappeared with Ray. She took Joy and me to the neighbor's house and left us, saying that Daddy would pick us up later. Bess then took Baby Ray by bus to her home in Texas. When Daddy got home and realized that Baby Ray had been kidnapped, he went to her parents in Texas and found them there. Ray was safe. Daddy returned with Ray and filed for divorce. Unable to have children herself, Bess had only married him to get a son.

Daddy never talked much about it; all we knew until we were older was that Ray had returned after a short absence and that Bess wouldn't be around anymore. I wonder how different Ray's life would have been had he been raised by someone who treasured him. It couldn't have been any worse.

Three children for a single man was too much, so we were sent back to live with our mother while Daddy finished OCS. Whatever she thought, she did take us back. Before he could finish, however, it was discovered that he had contracted tuberculosis while stationed in the Panama Canal Zone. He was shipped to Arizona because back then they believed the desert climate helped cure TB.

While we were with our mother she was trying to work at the Tallahassee courthouse as a secretary and take care of us too. She couldn't handle that any more than Daddy could. We were three burdens for both of them.

Our mother was a beautiful woman. She was also a vain woman, but even as an adult I didn't acknowledge that. Much of my life was spent trying to be as beautiful, as talented, and as appealing as she was. I thought I could earn her love and approval if I became just like her. I didn't realize that no matter what I did or became, I could never be beautiful, well mannered, or talented in her eyes. It wasn't until decades later that I finally acknowledged her inability to love anyone except herself. By then I was pretty well boxed in with scars.

When Daddy got his orders to travel to a sanatorium in Arizona, he first came back east to his sister's house in Sopchoppy, Florida, to say good-bye to us. I remember that even at that age I was afraid to be alone with him, although I didn't know why. He traveled to Sopchoppy, and Joy, Ray, and I were brought into the darkened bedroom there to say good-bye to him. He lay pale-faced, with big dark circles under his eyes and the sheets pulled up over his long thin frame.

My aunt left, and only Joy, Ray, and I remained in the room with him. I felt afraid. Daddy called me over to tell him good-bye. I didn't want to go. Before, he had been doing things to me I didn't like. Somehow they seemed wrong even though it was my daddy doing them. He said I had to say good-bye as I'd not see him for a long, long time. Reluctantly, I went. As I stood beside him his hand snaked around my back, into my panties and between my legs, where he began touching me in front. I tried to pull away, but he held me fast. Just then Aunt Mary walked into the room and said, "Slim, what are you doing?" and he said, "I'm checking to see if she wet her pants." I haughtily drew myself up to my full diminutive self and proclaimed, "I don't wet my pants; I'm a big girl now." True, when I was frightened for myself or someone else, I did wet myself, but never otherwise. Aunt Mary took me by one hand and Joy by the other and said, "Come along, children; your father needs a rest, for he has a long trip ahead of him." I often wondered if she knew or suspected and was trying to protect us. I don't think she really wanted to know.

The three of us were ushered into another room where we were served cake and red Jell-O that jiggled "like Santa's belly," as we were told. It took our minds off events in the bedroom. Some of my father's sisters stayed in touch with my mother through the years and always spoke kindly of her to us. Perhaps they knew some of what she'd gone through.

While he was in the army, Daddy sent support money for us so Mother could make ends meet. When he was medically discharged from the service, however, there was no more support money, or not much. That was when our mother sent us to Grandma and Grandpa's, which was a blessing, as we'd been traumatized by some really bad sitters, especially the last one who took us to a funeral home and threatened us with death. A new phase of life was about to open for us.

Chapter Three

GRANDMA AND GRANDPA LOVE

Solid, unconditional love first entered my life when I was four years old. Humor tagged along on its heels, although I was not to recognize it for years to come. As a skinny, energetic little kid, I failed to see that my creativity drove me to new adventures, which sometimes hugged the edge of danger. In a year's time I probably took ten years off my grandparents' life expectations!

In maturity, I recognized that my happiest days of childhood were those at Grandma and Grandpa Love's farm. In fact, they were the only happy days of childhood I remembered.

Ray and Ollie Love were highly respected farmers who lived in Stewart, Florida, a small rural farming community southwest of Tallahassee. By the time my younger sister Joy and baby brother Ray and I were left with Grandma and Grandpa we had pretty much made the rounds of places to stay and all the baby-sitters were used up. As a last resort, we were taken to Grandma and Grandpa's, my mother's parents.

It wasn't until years later that I saw the situation with adult eyes. Why did two people nearing the far side of middle age agree to take us in? What did they think of a daughter who was shaking free of her responsibility to us? What depths of love drove them to accept us so unconditionally?

Excepting Samuel Whitmore when I was seventeen, this was the only place in my first twenty-three years of living where I had felt loved, accepted, and secure. I would not feel that again until I married Ron, following the raw, open, still-oozing wound that was my first experience of marriage.

The last baby-sitter we had before we went to the farm was the worst. Not only did she mercilessly hit us, but she also caused Joy and me to dread sleep because of nightmares we began having. She had a friend who died, and she wanted to go to the viewing, so she left Ray with another friend and took us with her. At the funeral home she suddenly seemed obsessed. She took us individually and held us over the coffin. "See her? That's what will happen to you if you don't do what I say! You will die!" she hissed as she gave us a head-rattling shake. After that, both Joy and I often woke up screaming "I don't want to die!" or "Please don't put me in the box with the dead lady!"

Of course, Mother ignored our tales of being hit, shaken, and hung like a piece of meat over the dead woman's box. Finally, though, she mentioned it to a neighbor who had been at the funeral, and the neighbor corroborated our story and added that she thought the baby-sitter was sometimes beating us. Mother finally believed us! Not because of what we said, but because a grown-up told her. Kids don't have much of a chance to be believed in an adult world. Best forget it or take your lumps; just don't expect anyone to believe what you tell them. It was an early lesson in keeping my mouth shut that proved to be disastrous in years to come when a cry for help might have meant salvation. Finally Mother believed us and dismissed "the Witch." That's when we were taken to the farm.

Mother had a Tallahassee town apartment and a lifestyle to fit it. Whenever she came to visit us she always wore new clothes and shoes and had her hair coifed to perfection. I guess she felt that her job as a secretary at the courthouse required expensive clothes. We learned later that she had caught the eye of the governor's son and was dating him. She didn't tell him she had children. She didn't have to; we were moved to the farm about that time. At first, she visited us on weekends. After a while she didn't come so much, and her money didn't seem to stretch far enough to provide for us.

When she came to see us she was always splendidly groomed, garbed elegantly, and smelled like some famous princess from an exquisite faraway land. She was a very beautiful woman with jet black hair, white skin, and eyes as blue as the ocean. Joy and I both tried to imitate her. Slender and always beautifully dressed, she really was stunning, but she was also a vain woman who gave little time or thought to anyone save herself. She did have beautiful manners, which she taught us, but the eyes of reality could see she was just a beautiful but empty woman who didn't like the farm. Starchily dressed and wearing perky little hair ribbons, we would wait impatiently for her to come on weekends.

Grandma spent a great deal of time preparing us for Mother. She was pushed by the love our mother could not give. Perhaps she hoped it would rub off on Mother. It must have involved a lot of work, first washing and starching our clothes and then ironing them with the flat iron. And of course we had to have a bath before she got there, which meant much labor for Grandma and Grandpa both. If Mother had come on weekends and taken care of us, washing and ironing our clothes, giving us baths (all the water had to be carried to the washtub by hand), and helping financially to support us, they might have been able to keep us. Instead, she was busy making herself look acceptable. She really wanted to stay in town and go out with her boyfriend on the weekends and forget that she had three little children. Science has yet to understand how someone from the same gene pool, raised in one environment, can be so inverse on the poles of personality and taste from her parents.

Besides providing for us, our grandparents also had one remaining daughter at home. BeBe, their last child and my mother's sister, was in eighth grade. Certainly, she couldn't be expected to care full-time after school for three lively youngsters, ages five, four, and two, but with Grandma working it meant someone must be hired to look after us.

That's when Old Sam came into our lives. She was an ancient black woman, hired to stay at the farmhouse with us while Grandpa farmed and Grandma worked at the college. Sam was so old, all bent over and skin and bones. Her hair was white as snow, piled in a bun on top of her head. It didn't matter that her teeth were mostly all gone or that the remaining ones were yellow from chewing tobacco and snuff. She dipped snuff out of the little can that was always in her pocket. We came to love Old Sam, who taught us all about voodoo dolls and black magic. I learned to imitate her well; to walk with a shuffle all leaned over and to sit with vigor. I could talk like Old Sam in an accented dialect and could cuss like her too. I'm the only one who picked up on all those things, perhaps because I was older, but one evening when summer heat sat so heavy on our chests you could almost lick the flower-scented air like an ice cream cone, I tried to impress the grown-ups by showing them how I could spit way, way across the yard. When the spit effort feebled, I cussed some good Old Sam words. That's when it was decided that Old Sam must go. What she had been teaching us was not considered desirable for children—according to adults who were unable to view the world with a child's eyes. Our child's eyes thought Ole Sam was marvelously extraordinary!

"Sam" had been kind to us, and of course I didn't want her to leave. She taught us many wonderful things, like drawing faces on our knees. Since we'd never had a doll, she taught us how to wrap a blanket around our leg when we went to bed, with the knee face sticking out. That way, we could see the face and hold it like we would a doll and rock it to sleep. The rocking usually put us to sleep too, which, I suspect, was part of Old Sam's intentions.

One day when I woke up crying from a bad dream she picked me up and held me in the old rocking chair on the porch beside the washbasin where Grandpa washed when he came in, evenings. It was the first time I could ever remember someone holding me, besides Grandma and Grandpa.

Even though she was gone, we continued to make our knee dolls and never forgot the time Old Sam was in our lives. That year at Christmas Joy and I heard of Santa for the first time and excitedly put cookies out on a plate for him.

On Christmas morning Joy and I were given our very first doll, Betsy Wetsy! She was made of rubber, was about a foot high, and would wet her pants and drink with a bottle. Ray got a little wagon we could pull Betsy Wetsy in, Ray also got a tool box with a metal hammer and a little saw. Joy and I got a green Depression glass tea set.

Later, while dinner was cooking, we took the tea set around the house and put it beneath the big brick chimney where the moss grew on the wall and up the bricks. "That's how you know which way is north," Grandpa taught us. "It's where the moss grows thickest." Joy and I went in to ask Grandma if we could have some cookies or water to have a tea party. We heard a crashing, banging sound and ran outside to see Little Ray standing proudly by the tea set with his hammer in his hand. The tea set was in shards except for one tiny little green cup, which Grandma preserved in her living room as long as she and

Grandpa lived. Ray didn't get spanked for that; he didn't know what he was doing. He just did what you were supposed to do with a hammer. I can still see that little green tea set. As for Betsy Wetsy, she had a good long life and lasted until we moved to Arizona. Betsy died some years and several moves later when I was operating on her, and I buried her in a small barren backyard in Phoenix, Arizona. She died during a heart operation. I had heard that if you could locate a doll's heart and hold it in your hands it meant she would love you forever. I yearned to be loved like that; but Betsy died on the operating table without me ever finding her heart. It seemed that all the things I loved died or went away, like the green tea set or Old Sam or my mother.

After Old Sam left, Grandpa had to watch us and try to farm too. We didn't have any other baby-sitters. As I was the oldest at four, I was responsible for what the other two did. When Baby Ray ate dirt, I was spanked with Grandpa's hand—not a belt or razor strap—for not watching him. Grandpa said I was supposed to be taking care of him. The spanking was to reinforce "my sense of responsibility." It was a gentle spanking, but I never forgot it. I got a lot of hand spanks at Grandpa's knee that year, but I earned every one, and most times, I knew it. I somehow sensed that when Grandpa spanked me it was really because he loved me and wanted me to learn something. My sense of responsibility developed a lot that year, both from being on and from being across my grandfather's knee.

Later, as I grew up, I was always trying to please adults. I learned after we left the farm that if you keep the big people happy, there will be less beatings with hand, belt, or fist. With Grandpa there were no beatings; only gentle spankings that hurt my pride more than my backside. I wanted to please him out of love, not fear. Fear came later from hands and fists other than Grandpa's.

Usually I knew why I was being spanked, but there was one time I truly didn't realize I had been bad. It was a lazy summer day with nothing much to do. Even the worms were too warm to wiggle. I was supposed to be watching Joy and Ray. The chickens out by the henhouse were scratching halfheartedly in the dry dust of the day. I watched them lazily at first; then my interest perked up. "Look at those chickens. Let's us try to lay an egg like them!" In an innocent attempt to entertain them I had us all clambering onto the chicken fence. We sat there quite a while, teetering like floppy rags on a clothesline trying to stay up without pins. Occasionally we'd slip off and climb back on, waiting for one of us to lay the golden egg. Nothing happened; not white, speckled, brown, or golden. Slowly we began to realize that it wasn't going to work. That's when I got the next idea: taking over the chicken house! These ideas came to me sort of like leaves forming on a spring-struck tree. They just bloomed out, fuller and fuller. I proceeded to throw all the chickens out of their house, and we climbed onto the roost like the new proprietors we were. This was serious business—we were going to lay some eggs and had to find the perfect location to do it! We sat and sat, but all we laid was one broken shell of expectations. No eggs. We were very discouraged.

My four-year-old city-bred mind didn't know that chicken coops were notoriously full of chicken lice. When we emerged, straw-haired, scratching, and well covered with chicken poo, we were met with utter dismay. Silence was never more thickly ominous. Finally, our grandparents stumbled into movement as if they still couldn't believe their eyes. Grandpa fetched the big metal washtub, placed it on the porch, and went down to the spring for water. Then he went out back to bring up some firewood. Grandma heated up the water. It took quite a while. We sat around buck naked in the hot summer day, which felt freezing in the chilly, disapproving atmosphere, still uncertain what was so wrong. Finally we were all dipped into the bath. The silence still held, tying us as surely as cords to some blatant misdemeanor. We each got a bath. Over and over we got baths. Our heads were washed with kerosene and then rinsed before the burn could reach our scalp. Three times the kerosene was applied before the scissors appeared and Joy and I lost our long tresses for a new bobbed look. It sure was a lot of fuss over a few chickens.

We weren't allowed in the house until we had been thoroughly bathed and deloused. Saturday night was our usual bath night, but this week was different. It was a lot of extra work for two old people who had their days carefully laid out. Grandpa had to go down to the spring and lug up bucket after bucket of water. Grandma had to build a fire outdoors and heat the water in a big pot before she put it in the washtub. They had to scrub us three times with kerosene and then wash us again. It was an enormous job and had taken most of the rest of the day with both grandparents working hard. No wonder it meant a spanking! They said I was supposed to be watching Joy and Ray. I was watching. In fact I thought I'd been entertaining them, but apparently it was not parentally approved entertainment. At least Grandpa's hand certainly didn't feel like a stamp of approval.

There were also times when I deserved a spanking and Grandpa's understanding nature overrode the punishment. I was forever taking things apart. Once I took apart our Easter baskets to see if I could weave them back together. I couldn't. They were the only Easter baskets we ever got.

Another time I heard someone ask Grandpa where his watch was, and he replied that it had quit running. I knew he treasured that watch, so one day I sat down and took it apart. The trouble was that my four years of experience didn't include watch repair. I couldn't get it back together, and neither could Grandpa.

"Why'd you take my watch apart?" he asked.

"Because I wanted to fix it for you," I whispered. Grandpa didn't spank me then. He understood that I was trying to do something nice for him. But I always felt sad that I couldn't fix it. I knew how much he loved that watch.

Another time I can recall sadness was when Grandma was given a gift of three soft-looking soap lambs for us. They smelled like the outdoors and were so fluffy looking. I begged all day to take a bath that night. Finally, even though it wasn't Saturday, Grandpa got the big washtub down and Grandma filled it with hot water that she had heated over the fire. It was so exciting! I splashed and screamed for a while, enjoying each scented moment. Suddenly I realized that my fluffy white lamb was just a plain old bar of soap. The lambiness of it had disappeared. I let out a grieved wail, and tears flowed like Niagara Falls. That lamb was forever gone, and for some strange reason neither Joy nor Ray wanted to give me theirs, even though I cajoled and promised them many things. It was a grievous loss to me but taught me to treasure what I had and to use it wisely, because like all the other things life handed out, it wouldn't last.

One particular time Grandpa spanked me proper was when I climbed to the top of the mule-driven sugarcane grinder. I tied Joy and Ray to the place where the mules went round, climbed to the top, and perched precariously on the edge of the hopper where the cane is dropped in to be ground. "Gee-haw!" I yelled, swishing a stick in the air and adding some of Old Sam's favorite four-letter words. I didn't know that the Gee-haw words meant "left" and "right," but I knew that they were words Grandpa used when he was grinding cane. Had Joy and Ray been able to move the poles, I could have been crushed in the hopper. Out in the fields, Grandpa heard me yelling. As he came racing in from the fields he could see me straddled across the grinder. I probably took a few months off his life right then. Had I fallen, I would likely have died.

Another time Grandpa's intervention saved a life—or broken bones at least—was when we decided that, with a little help, Ray could fly. I loved the smell of the barn, all dusty with sun motes dancing in the air, smelling of hay. There was a wooden ladder nailed to the inside wall. If I climbed up it I would come to the hay window where they lifted hay into the mow. Standing there, peering out the window, I was queen of all I surveyed. It was about two stories up, so I could look out over fields and trees and sky that stretched endlessly. It was a magic world! A rope and pulley hung from a wooden arm extended above the hay window. That rope gave me an idea.

Joy and I decided we would take Ray up the ladder, tie him, and throw him out the window so he would drop and swing just like he was flying. I had to lean way out to get the rope used to pull bales of hay up into the hayloft, but finally I succeeded. It never occurred to me that one slip, one moment of overbalancing, would mean a probably fatal fall. Now we were ready for little Ray. We planned to tie him to the pulley rope and push him out the window, where he would "fly." Of course we considered the odds and confidently decided that he would be safe because we would tie him well, which we did, of course. But little Ray didn't think it was a "matter of course." He began protesting. He didn't want to go up the ladder any further, so we tried simultaneously pulling and pushing—one of us above; one below. He screamed so loud that Grandpa heard him way out in the fields. His timely rescue of Ray probably saved him from serious injury or even death. I knew why I was getting spanked that time; however, secretly I always thought we could have made Ray fly.

Never again, after leaving the farm, was I to receive that gentle kind of spanking that hurt your feelings more than your bottom. They were never abusive or overly hard; they were intended to teach a lesson, and I always knew the reason for them. They are among my forever memories, and somehow they now nestle in my heart more like love letters from the past than past punishments. They were measured moments that turned into treasured memories.

Chapter Four

MY GRANDMA AND GRANDPA'S DAYS

Busy as he was, Grandpa still found time to teach me things. Grandpa had built the barns, outhouse, cane grinder, and sheds out of wood taken from the farm. Once he showed me how to make a real log cabin. He was building a log shed by himself, with logs from his land, and as he built (with me always underfoot, full of curiosity and questions), he taught me how to notch a log and fit it into another log and how to lift it up to build the wall. I would then get little sticks and try to build my "own log cabin." I became Miss Fixit at an early age, only I frequently unfixed more than I fixed, like Grandpa's watch.

While we were working, Grandpa would tell me stories about his life, like the time he lost his eye when another boy put it out as they playing bow and arrow. After that, he always had to wear a blue glass eye. It fascinated me to watch Grandpa put his eye in. I asked him to do it so often it's a wonder his socket didn't wear down to a frazzled flap. Patiently, he always complied. The eye was a big white orb that he slid into the socket. When it was in you could only see a little bit of the white and his blue painted pupil. I was enchanted with the whole operation.

I guess I thought a lot about the story of how he lost his eye, because one day when we had some boiled peanuts on hand and things were rather quiet, Grandma and Grandpa suddenly heard Joy screaming. They rushed into the room where she lay on her back with me straddling her, trying to insert a peanut in her eye. It was a small one, really.

"Hold still and let me put your eye in!" I was ordering her in a loud five-year-old voice as they reached us.

Another spanking. My curiosity often put me in perilous positions.

Looking back, I think some of our youthful antics may have contributed to Grandpa's stroke. My grandparents had no conveniences, and I am sure the care of three small children in addition to their own BeBe was more than they bargained for.

I remember the house well. Like its owners, it welcomed you with outstretched veranda arms hugging interlacing morning glories. Their delicate colors and green leaves contrasted sharply with the white paint of the house. Beautiful pots of asparagus ferns placed all across the porch graced our serenity with additional beauty. Sometimes at night Grandma and Grandpa would sit on the front veranda in the rockers. Grandma shelled peas or beans while Grandpa shucked corn, and we kids would chase one another in the yard and catch fireflies.

That wraparound porch still reminds me of how wrapped around we were with Grandma and Grandpa's love. Their love was the life-raft that carried me to shores of survival in years to come. It was both a standard to carry into the future and a reminder that someone had once found me lovable. Perhaps because they were younger Joy and Ray didn't remember as well, and so our year with Grandma and Grandpa didn't influence them the way it did me. It always gave me a ray of hope to live by. But as they grew up Joy and Ray didn't seem to remember the love they had received and the hope it gave. Joy has now been married seven times, and Ray has cirrhosis of the liver.

The bedroom walls in Aunt BeBe's room were sun-yellow, with curtains of sheer white. If you were very good, Aunt BeBe would let you take a turn sleeping with her in her room, where you could catch the rise of the early morning sun climbing above the bedroom window. Once when it was my turn to stay in Aunt Bebe's room I planned a big surprise with my four-year-old mental antics. After spending a long time catching them, I filled Aunt Bebe's room with fireflies. I thought with so many "firefly candles" we could see at night to read by firefly light. Aunt BeBe was not amused by all the flying insects, and neither was Grandma. I thought they were beautiful.

We had no conveniences, but as kids we didn't know the difference. Without electricity, we used kerosene lamps and had an icebox to keep things cool. Grandma cooked over a cast-iron wood stove and baked in its oven. The hot water we had came from the reservoir of the stove. We always were dressed neat and clean when we sallied forth from the farm, and that meant a lot of work for Grandma. All our water had to be lugged up from the spring, and all our clothes had to be ironed with her flat iron set on a hot stove to warm. Maintaining the house meant endless work just to keep things going. Every time it was cold and every time Grandma cooked or baked there had to be a fire in the cook stove. Fires meant wood, which meant cutting, hauling, splitting, and carrying. Grandpa would say, "A fire warms you four times: once when you cut it, once when you haul it out of the woods, once when you split it, and once when you carry it in." I figured taking it out warmed you four times too. Once when you emptied the ashes into a metal container, once when you carried them out, once when you spread them over the garden, and once when you had to sweep up the mess you had made.

But there was something about fires that made them worth the work. They talked to you, snapping and crackling. Light from the fireplace balleted across burning wood as heat felt for our fingers and warmed winter-filled limbs. We all gathered close to the fireplace then, and when bedtime came there was no dawdling; we rushed to get under the pile of blankets as soon as we walked into the unheated bedrooms. Often at night I would listen to the fire's friendly conversations from my observation post in the bedroom.

Even though the house demanded a lot of work, it was a house of warmth. It was a place to explore ever new wonders of nature, to learn useful things like how to tie brothers to baling ropes or how to "make cane syrup" or about chicken houses and their inhabitants. But most of all, it was a house of love and acceptance and security. Days passed like smooth syrup. Sometimes the flow was interrupted by pranks and spankings, but there was never any doubt that we were loved. That certainty remained in my heart and memory as if someone knew how essential those memories were to become to my survival in the future when life became cold, bleak, and dark. I would hug their light and warmth to my heart like the pas de deux turns of flickering firelight warming darkened rooms.

Chapter Five

UNCONDITIONALLY LOVED

At Grandma and Grandpa's, everyone worked to do what they could. Only little Ray was exempt from work.

I baby-sat (watched) Joy and Ray, and both Joy and I helped fetch and carry. We helped do dishes and set things on the table, and I was always following Grandpa around, imitating him, seeing what I could do to help, and just generally complicating his life. He never let on that I was anything but delightful company.

It wasn't much later that Grandpa had his first stroke. All this time my mother was living in Tallahassee and could have come out to care for us on weekends. As I said before and still believe, if she had helped Grandma and Grandpa, they probably could have continued to keep us. I guess she just got tired of being a mom. She cared more about making herself acceptable to others than accepting us. But we couldn't see that, then. To a child, mothers can do no wrong. We saw only the good in her. Most of my adult life was spent trying to measure up to my mother, to be as beautiful, dress as well, take care of my hair as well … even as a grown-up I was not able to face the fact that our mother never loved us. When she was with us BL (before lice), she did my and Joy's hair in beautiful ringlets and curls. She played with us like she would a doll, but she never took part in the responsibilities and work that three children entailed.

Little Ray was two by then and wore little corduroy overalls over his shirts. Grandma made Ray a stick hobby horse with a face from one of Grandpa's socks, which he rode everywhere around the farm. Mother never had much to do with Ray. It was as if she could never forgive him for his painful birth. He grew up without a mother's love.

The effects were devastating, in spite of his year with Grandma and Grandpa. He was too young for their unconditional love to set up in the custard of his forming character.

There were so many ways my grandparents showed their unconditional love for us—many of them unrealized by me until much later. I'm sure they were unpaid for taking care of us. Most likely my father was not contributing to our welfare, and certainly after a while there was no money forthcoming from Mother either, so all our expenses of clothing and food must have come from their own pockets. It meant that Grandma would have to go to work to provide for us. She found a job in Tallahassee on weekdays.

Whenever she was home, good smells always came from the kitchen and the big old farmhouse was always fresh and clean. Life was ordered and neat, and we all felt loved there. No matter what changes were made because of us, we were never made to feel unwanted or resented. My happiness had no boundaries.

As I've said, we used fireplaces for heat and an ice box for cooling food. One day when the Florida sun beat down on fields and house and the summer land was heat-smothered, I turned up missing. I'd been missing about three hours when everyone was called in to search for me. They searched the woods around the house and also the old well and the barns. Finally someone got thirsty and went into the kitchen. That was the day the iceman came. The big old icebox had a wooden plug underneath that could drain melted ice water. I always followed the ice man in, watching him carry the block of ice on his shoulder with a big black pair of tongs. He always gave me ice chips; sometimes they'd have tiny pieces of sawdust on them.

The thirsty person entered the kitchen, and there, all over the floor of the kitchen, were food jars, milk, and a little heap of clothes. Everything sat out. Puzzled, he opened the door of the old icebox, and there I was, stark naked and blue, shivering, and chattering, "I'm cold, I'm cold!" The icebox drain had been left off, and that's what had saved me from suffocation. I was unaware of God's touch in my life then, but it has happened so many times since that I have no doubt about it: God has His hand on my life. But then, He always loves and longs to hold anyone who will let Him!

I must have been a handful then, always investigating everything—even icebox interiors—and chasing the chickens "which frightened and made them skinny," I was told over and over. They said it made the old hens too tough for Sunday dinner. I followed Grandpa almost everywhere; however, there were some times when I wouldn't follow him at all.

He loved to hunt. Sometimes when he wasn't working in the fields or baby-sitting or going to town, he would get his gun and go to the woods to shoot squirrels and rabbits and wild ducks over the pond. As much as I loved Grandpa I couldn't bear to go with him then. Instead I would run to the bedroom and crawl under the bed with my hands over my ears. I still could hear the shots, though, and I'd know that some animal had given his life so we could eat. I'd lie under the bed and sob, fingers covering my ears every time I heard the rifle blast. It didn't bother Joy or Ray, but I still remember the grief I felt for the fallen animals of the world, little knowing that in a few more months I would feel like one of them.

Sometimes when Grandpa took a load of corn to market into Stewart, I'd ride into town with him on the seat of the big old wooden wagon pulled by the mule. Those rides were magical ones to me, with just Grandpa and me in the wagon and the old horses shuffling along. The wagon would go bumpity-bump, and I would imitate the squeaky sounds of the wheels with my mouth. I began doing this when we first visited Grandpa and Grandma when I was only eighteen months old. It always amused Grandpa to hear me.

I remember the day, even down to what I was wearing, when I went into town with Mother and Daddy in the car, because that is when I got my first beating. I began doing my "bumpity-bump" song. It always amused Grandpa, so I thought I would do it for them too. Daddy told me to stop it, and I did, but soon, forgetting, I was bumpity-humming again. Without a further word he stopped the car, yanked me out, took off his belt, and gave me a vicious beating that raised welts on my legs, buttocks, and back. The psychological trauma of that first beating, however, was the worst part. Perhaps that's why I can remember it at such an early age.

Grandpa enjoyed my bumpity–humming—or at least acted like he did—so we went merrily into town, horses snorting, me humming.

When he went in to get a haircut I went along, entertained by everything and everyone I saw. The barber shop was full of interesting things, and I watched men get shaved with a straight razor, get haircuts, and even get nose and ear haircuts. A lot of the men had their own shaving mugs hanging under their names from a hook driven into the wall. It was fascinating to go to town with Grandpa!

Grandpa lived for many years in a wheelchair after several strokes, and Grandma cared for him as she had for us. Grandma had an ample lap to climb on. Sometimes she'd hold us on the old porch swing and rock back and forth. Later she sat there alone with Grandpa beside her in his wheelchair to keep her company.

Certainly those times must have been hard for Grandma, but the only time I ever saw her cry was when they had a party for us before we left. Everyone was there, and they had a big feast. Suddenly Grandma covered her face with her starched white apron and ran inside, saying she "just couldn't stand to see those babies go."

A month after Grandpa died, Grandma died of pneumonia. The doctor said that if he ever saw anyone die of a broken heart, it was Grandma. They're both buried in Stewart Cemetery. The big old farmhouse and lands were sold off.

All their lives my grandparents attended the little Methodist church by the graveyard, and I still go back to Stewart, Florida, to visit that old cemetery whenever I can. There, I once again find the only bright memories of my childhood. I pray over those memories then, blessing two aged grandparents who always had enough love for one more child … or two, or three.

Chapter Six

JEAN AND DADDY

I next saw my father back in Florida a year after he left for Arizona and the TB sanatorium. He got off a bus, tall and slender, on crutches and wearing a full cast on his leg, to take the three of us back with him to live in Arizona. After Grandma said she could no longer keep us, Mother wrote to him, saying, "Come and get these brats or I'm going to put them in an orphanage," or so Daddy told us. By then he had been cured and given a medical discharge from the army.

After Daddy remarried, he wrote my real mother a letter giving her his change of address in case she ever needed to reach him. In the meantime, Jean, his new wife, became pregnant with Dolly. It wasn't too much later that our mother contacted Daddy with the "Come and get 'em!" message. By then Joy and I had regrown our (chicken) lice-lost tresses. We were reaching the lanky stage. A photograph taken before we left shows two little girls seated on Grandma and Grandpa's porch, surrounded by morning glory vines trailing up the sides of the house on strings Grandpa put up. We were dressed in white stiff starched blouses with ruffles and little wool pleated plaid skirts, our feet still in white high-top Buster Browns and white socks. Little Ray wore his red corduroy overalls and shirt and rode his beloved hobby stick horse made from Grandpa's sock. I was five by then.

We had been at our grandparents' less than a full year. We posed in an old child's rocking chair in front of Grandma and Grandpa's house. It was not yet autumn-cool, for Grandma's pots of ferns still sat on the sides of the porch stoop. As soon as the weather began to chill Grandpa always carried the double huge pots of ferns in a wheelbarrow to "winter" by the brook, at the spring. Old oak trees hung heavy with

Spanish moss, but the yard trees were losing their leaves. There was an autumn feel in the air.

Did you know Spanish moss is not a parasite as so many people think? It is an epiphyte, living on air; not sucking the life out of the trees that give it support and shelter. However, for all its beauty it still can slowly kill a tree from its sheer amount and density. You don't have to be a parasite to kill. Our tormentors were not parasites either, but they nevertheless managed to squeeze and strangle our childhood years by indifference and deliberate cruelty.

Life hinges on such slender circumstances. Had we grown up there on the farm, my life would have been entirely different. Instead, my mother, happy to leave us at the farm, had to find some other way of dealing with us when her own parents became too feeble to shoulder the load of our care.

After we left, Grandpa had two more strokes. He lived for many years in a wheelchair and Grandma cared for him. Even in his wheelchair he could make Grandma feel special. One day before we left, she was fussing about not getting her hair done when company caught her with it "messy looking."

"You shore don't look messy to me," Grandpa declared. "In fact, you look beautiful to me, Babe." Grandma's smile turned her wrinkles into a million little sun-rayed lines right then. He always knew how to make her feel beautiful and loved. He made us feel the same way—precious, valued, and beautiful.

It was nighttime when Daddy arrived to take us to his mother and daddy's in nearby Sopchoppy, Florida, for a few days. It was a new adventure for us. I remember Grandma Jerry mending on the porch while we hung on an old tire swing in the yard. I also remember making hairdos for us out of Spanish moss that hung low on the trees. (That may be when we learned that chiggers inhabit Spanish moss!) Soon we learned that we would be staying with Daddy and his new wife from now on, which meant that we would have a new home, far away from everyone we knew.

About a year after he arrived in Arizona, Daddy was pronounced "cured" and went to work in Phoenix at a restaurant called the Java Café. There he met Jean, a divorcée with two sons, Lee and Gil, who worked there as a waitress. Gil was six months younger than me, and Lee was seven years older. Lee and Gil were enrolled in a series of daycares and with baby-sitters. Jean's former husband Strong, the father of Lee and Gil, had been a policeman. Daddy and Jean went together for a short time and then married. After their marriage they bought a house on Orange Road, in Phoenix, Arizona. It was in a little suburban community with farmland nearby. This is where we would be taken to meet our new stepmother.

One of my last memories of Grandma Jerry is the evening before we left. She took a pot of white cream from the refrigerator. She sprinkled it with sugar and gave us crusty home baked bread. She then showed us how to break off the bread and dip into the sweet cream. The taste was like wild summer roses: subtle, sweet, and lasting, and totally fat-free, of course. That was to be her final treat to us. The next day we left for Arizona. I was never to see her again. She died while we were in Arizona.

So began our journey by bus back to Phoenix with Daddy and his broken leg. The bus trip was hard. At the bus station strangers were protesting to Daddy, saying, "How in the world can you handle three children with your leg in a full cast and on crutches?" Passengers and bus drivers all pitched in to help, carrying Ray and our luggage. People would place us in our seats, under Daddy's observant eye. At rest stops, Daddy would ask nice-looking ladies if they would take Joy and me to the bathroom while he changed Ray's diapers. Joy was blonde-haired and blue-eyed and looked like a little princess. Ray had our mother's bright blue eyes and looked like a cute, cuddly doll. Different people helped feed and cuddle them, but I was sort of on my own. No longer cute, I'd grown skinny and gangly legged, with ears that stuck straight out from my head. I looked like a skinned rat. How I longed for one of those pretty ladies to notice me and maybe even hold me a moment on her lap, but no one did. We rode forever, it seemed, with nothing to do but sleep and fidget. Somehow we made it through that wretched, long trip.

When we arrived in Phoenix it was late at night. We were about to meet three strangers who would play a definite negative part in shaping our future. Our stepmother Jean, Gil, and Lee picked us up at the bus station. We were tired, exhausted from the grueling trip, plunked down in a strange place with a brand new family. It was a lot to absorb. Jean, our stepmother, was intimidating: very large, she wore her hair severely parted in the middle, pulled straight back, and twisted into a bun on the back of her head. I felt afraid just meeting her.

After we got to the house we were given bananas to eat. Never having seen a banana before, I picked it up and bit into it, peel and all. Everyone laughed at me. Embarrassment stung my spirit like sandpaper skinning a peach. Hitherto, everything we'd had was farm-grown and cooked. Here, everything felt unfamiliar and strange. Soon we were put to bed in a strange new place. Always a light sleeper, I lay awake, hearing every noise. When daylight came, we were carelessly served a bowl of cold cereal and then sent outdoors. To this day I hate cold cereal. To me cold cereal says "unwelcome." That's certainly how we felt that morning … and as long as we lived there.

I guess our stepmother tried at first. Perhaps she was overwhelmed. She'd gone from two sons to two sons and being pregnant to two sons, pregnancy, and three more kids overnight! When they'd married they had not expected the sudden "gift" of three more to raise.

Sometime after our arrival, our stepmother was allowed to go to the hospital and had Baby Dolly. Her time demands were even greater after that.

One day shortly before Dolly was born, someone gave our stepmother free movie tickets, and she took the five of us to see *Fantasia* by Walt Disney. It probably would have been wonderful if shorter, but by its long end we were all fidgeting and fussing. After that, for reasons unclear to me, Gil and Lee began to torment us whenever they could. Perhaps they were jealous of the new interlopers on their mother's time. But it wasn't just the boys who tormented us. My stepmother did too. Later, when we saw a picture of Dumbo the Elephant, my stepmother said, "That's your name, Jeanne; you're Dumbo the Elephant. And your ears are just like his … big!" All the kids began to laugh, tweaking my ears, which I already was so self-conscious of. My hair was now pulled straight back and parted down the middle in two long pigtails, which exposed my big ears, sticking straight out from my skull like two handles on a jug. My face, from staying outside all day in the hot Arizona sun, was covered with freckles, which only served to somehow emphasize my funny ears. Stepmother kept telling me that I looked like a guinea hen "pooted" (pooped) in my face. What really hurt was that Gil would go to school and repeat this and all the kids would then pick it up and tease me: "Pooted guinea hen; greckled wreckled." It wasn't until years later that I learned that Malaysians think freckles are really angels' kisses. Had I known, it might have helped, although the main thing that hurt wasn't the freckles or my ears but the fact that a grown-up person who should have known better enjoyed teasing so cruelly.

After we ate our cereal in the morning we were to make our beds and go outside to entertain ourselves until called to eat at noon, Gil and Lee were at school, but by now my stepmother was saddled with a new baby as well as three preschoolers. Quite a change from her quiet days before our arrival! By sending us outdoors, she could get back to her previous quietude, somewhat. We didn't realize how unsupervised we were; as long as we didn't bother our stepmother we were absolutely free until lunchtime.

As time went on she learned how to have even more time for herself by appointing me, at age five, her baby-sitter. She'd have me sit and hold Baby Dolly in my arms so she could get things done. I didn't mind. I loved Dolly. She was like a real live doll, and I would spend hours just holding her. My stepmother wasn't so mad at me when I held Dolly, since it helped her. During the day, as long as Joy and I were outside with Dolly, she was free of caring for any of us. Soon Dolly was so used to me that she began to cry for me if I wasn't holding her. At age six, I held her on my hip and carried her around while my stepmother hung clothes or whatever she was doing.

One evening, with the family around, I was holding Baby Dolly in my skinny little arms when she suddenly reared backward. My arms were around her hips, so I didn't drop her, but she hung upside down. If I'd ever been told to hold onto her back I don't remember it. Daddy started screaming about supporting her back. He grabbed her from me and began to beat me with his razor strap until my kidneys seemed to collapse and urine ran down my legs. It was at times like these when I would still wet my pants. These were no "Grandpa spankings"; these were brutal beatings that raised welts on my legs and back and sometimes bled. Finally my stepmother stopped him, and he ordered me never to pick Dolly up again. For a couple of days Dolly cried and cried for me, so finally, while Daddy was gone, my stepmother handed her to me and told me to "take her; it's all right." I was afraid of Daddy, but since Stepmother said it was all right I believed her. I carried Dolly all day and played with her and entertained her. She laughed and cooed and loved me to rock her. It was a good day.

My six-year-old mind didn't realize that it was getting late. Afternoon shadows were striding across the blades of grass and creeping up our stucco house. It was time for Daddy to come home! When he stepped in the door, Dolly was on my hip. He saw it and grabbed the razor strap hanging on the wall. I screamed and nearly dropped Dolly, but then my stepmother intervened and told him she made me hold her. "She cries too much, otherwise," she said. It was one of the few times I remember my stepmother standing up for me. Daddy didn't spank me, and after that Dolly became my baby. As she grew I was her teacher and entertainment committee. I baby-sat every day. I kept her out of mischief and played games with her. Good-natured and laughing, she grew up secure in the love of someone only six years older than she was. It didn't seem to matter; she was loved and knew it. She was secure. Except for the year at Grandpa and Grandma's, we were never to know that kind of "you are loved" security.

Dolly was bald-headed until she was about two years old, so everyone thought she was a boy, Dolly's baldness didn't really present a problem, but it did set her apart. When a neighbor told Daddy that if he'd cover her head in mayonnaise and let it sit a while, hair would start coming in, he followed their advice. Dolly's head was basted in mayonnaise and a rubber shower cap placed over it for several hours. She was pretty comical looking with her shower cap wanting to slide around in the mayonnaise and slither down on her face! When the cap was removed and her head finally washed, she remained as bald as ever. So much for the mayonnaise treatment. It taught me something more about believing everything adults tell you.

Daddy had welded Dolly a metal rickshaw from old pipes. I hauled her around in it until she was too big; then she tried to put her baby dolls in it, but the metal pipes were too heavy for her to push. It was an ingenious idea, and had it been made of lighter materials, it would have been great. I remember that rickshaw because Daddy never made things like that for any of the three of us. Funny thing—I don't think we ever expected it. We had learned to expect nothing. It was a realistic expectation. I used to wonder what we three had done that made him treat us so differently from the others. He made me feel like the south end of a chicken headed north.

I guess when my mother received Daddy's letter saying he had remarried, she felt like she was getting nowhere in life. That was when she wrote Daddy telling him she was sick of raising brats and he could come get the three of us or she'd put us in an orphanage, because Grandma and Grandpa and Aunt BeBe couldn't take care of us anymore. With that letter, one part of our lives ended. A far different story would be written in bold letters on the pages of our hearts in the years to come. The best years of my childhood were now over, and I was about to enter a growing nightmare with a stepmother named Jean as a key player.

Chapter Seven

EXACT AND IMMEDIATE OBEDIENCE

We had only been in Arizona a few weeks. The bus ride back with Daddy was memory-fresh in our heads and our welcome still uncertain, but we had already made some friends. At least, that is what we called Jannie at the time, although later I would learn more of her cruel side than I ever wanted to know.

We had been told to be home by dark; that was about all the parental supervision we ever got. That slow dusky evening we had been playing in Jannie's field, having so much fun that we didn't notice the sun dropping lower and lower in the sky.

My stepmother claimed that she called us twice to come home. None of the five of us heard her. Suddenly we realized that the dusky sky was all ready giving birth to darkness. As one, we ran for home. Spooky shadows followed us across weedy fields and pasturelands as trees and bushes assumed weird patterns in the beginning silvered moonlight.

When we got to the house it was totally dark inside. No lights shone from any window to welcome us. There wasn't a single light anywhere in the house or out in the yard. A chill shook my body at the same time a premonition hit my mind. It was too still, too dark, too quiet. Something wasn't right. "Stop!" I alarmed. "I'm scared—something's wrong in there!" Lee, ignoring my fright, trooped right in; at twelve he was afraid of nothing. Gil followed. At six, I was the oldest of the three remaining children (Joy, Ray, and me), but I hesitated. No sounds came from inside, however, so there must not be any boogie men there. Hesitantly, I stepped inside. Suddenly from out of the stifling heat and oppressive darkness the shadows moved and Daddy loomed above me, razor strap in hand. He snatched me by my wire-thin arm and began beating me.

The strap hit with monotonous brutality, slashing across bare legs and thin back, cutting deep. My bladder became fluid as the terror progressed until finally urine ran down my leg to mingle with the blood. It scalded and stung the open cuts created by the strap. I almost never wet the bed. On the rare occasions when I did, I was beaten for it, yet Gil wet his every night without any punishment. Things like that are noticed and remembered by children. However, I didn't think of that as the strap continued to echo on my skin. The more I screamed the harder he slashed until, tiring, he turned on Joy and gave her some vicious licks. Then finally even little three-year-old Ray received his share of blows. It was "to teach us all a lesson." "Us all" meant the three of us; Gil and Lee never got spanked for anything. Their mother, our stepmother, wouldn't allow it. "But," she told Daddy, "since those three aren't mine, you can do whatever you want with them." And he did.

The immediate reason was usually some trumped-up charge that seemed to relieve his lust for brutality, but the overall effect—and purpose, I suspect—was to teach us fear, unquestioning, immediate raw fear. A few weeks before I had been a cherished child, secure in Grandma and Grandpa's love, never doubting that life was sweet and safe. Now my psyche had been irretrievably raped by new lessons forced on it. I was brutalized and impregnated with terror.

From then on, Joy, Ray, and I listened more fearfully and came if we even *thought* we were being called, no matter what we were doing. We dropped whatever it was that held our attention and ran for home in fear and trembling, never knowing what lay in wait when we arrived. We were taught, carefully taught, to "be afraid unless we obeyed." At least, obedience is what Daddy called it. To us the lesson was not about exact and immediate obedience; it was about fear. We responded instantly because we were so afraid. We lived with that fear all the time when we were home. It was a natural state of being for us, like curiosity or security or comfort is for many children. We were being trained to accept fear as a way of life. Quick learners, our goals turned to instant obedience coupled with a desire to stay as far away from our father as possible and to be as quiet as possible so he wouldn't notice us. Warfare would call it camouflage; we just thought of it as trying to fade into the background. Like any frightened animal, we learned that blending in with the background may mean salvation. But being a frightened animal was not enough to escape Daddy's rages, as we were soon to learn.

I entered first grade that fall. Lee, Gil, and I rode the school bus to town. Riding a bus that stopped just for us was very impressive, and I looked upon each day as a great adventure. As we traveled home at day's end I noticed a lot of kids jump off the bus and run into their homes, carrying their day's work of pictures, drawings, and penciled efforts as they called out to their mothers. I had already learned to enter quietly and to quickly become "camouflage." That day, however, when we got home, Stepmother was crying. Her eyes were red, and her sobs shuddered through our little house. I couldn't keep quiet. "What's wrong?" I asked, afraid to know and afraid not to know.

"We were fighting, and your daddy poured cement in my flower bed," she sobbed, and then, noticing it was I who asked, she snarled, "Now you shut up and get out. I don't want to see you in here again, Jeanne. Go on; out!"

I wandered outside. Daddy had been building a cement stanchion to milk the cow in, and he'd poured his leftover cement across the blooming zinnias and daisies, ruining her flowers. I looked at the cement, slopped carelessly into the flower bed, and then ambled toward the barn to see if the gray cat had had her kittens and to look at the new milking stanchion Daddy had so proudly designed and built.

What I saw turned my blood to ice shards that stabbed deep into the tissues of my forever-memories. The old gray ma cat had made a bed for her babies on a pile of straw and had begun delivering her litter of kittens when Daddy found her. He took his fury with Stepmother out on the cat. He didn't hear me enter the barn; his back was turned to me and he was hitting the old ma cat like he hit me; instead of a strap, however, he had a length of lead pipe in his hand. He kicked her full fat abdomen with his steel-toed safety boots and stomped at her with his heels. The barn was full of meows and cries of pain; there was blood splattered everywhere: on the new cement stanchion, the walls, and floor. Clumps of gray fur blew lazily in the air. The tiny pink blind kittens were lying on the floor being stomped on, and pieces of pink gore clung to walls and floor along with the blood.

I began crying and screaming, begging him to stop. "Oh, Daddy! Daddy! Please don't! Please stop, Daddy! Daddy, please!" His maniacal rage now centered on me, and he began yelling and coming for me, screaming that this is what he'd do to us if we ever got pregnant, if we ever disobeyed, if we ever … I turned and ran. The other kids were there too by then, and all of us were crying and screaming. In the midst of all the confusion somehow the old gray cat escaped and hid. But I knew that there was no hiding for me. Day after day I would have to face this man through all my growing-up years. I hated him then and feared him even more than before. If anything crossed this man he would fly into an insane rage, and woe to anyone or anything in his way.

Looking back I feel sure that this was the year I began to know what it was to live in fright. If it's true that "you have to be taught to be afraid," I am sure I was well taught the summer and fall of my first year in school, and I proved to be a quick learner.

Chapter Eight

MOTHER'S VISIT

With our arrivals in Phoenix, Daddy had gone overnight from caring for two boys to supporting five and a half kids. My real mother had a good job at the state capitol in Tallahassee, but she never sent any money for our support. Daddy worked days on one job and finally got a night job also. My stepmother stayed home.

Even at age six I had an uncanny sensitivity concerning situations and relationships. Thus I gradually became aware of an atmosphere of anger and resentment surrounding us like the miasma from a stagnant Florida swamp. Just as the hushed high humidity of swamps is unseeable but certainly feelable, I could sense a stultifying presence engulfing us, permeating all we did. To feel like "just another mouth to feed" is to feel devoid of usefulness, like discarded feathers from a freshly killed waterfowl, drifting without purpose, without reason for existence. We were like loose feathers blowing in the wind, trying to find another body to attach to. By having purpose, we would again become desirable enough to keep. Good behavior became our compensation, our excuse for being such burdens. We tried to please by learning to drop everything and come running when we were called. Daddy's razor strap was probably the prime motivator for that, however, truth be told!

Had his strap been applied to Lee and Gil it might not have hurt us so much, but there were different rules for "her kids" (Lee and Gil; "his kids" were Joy, Ray, and me) and "their kid," Dolly and later Baby John. As if it weren't bad enough to feel resented at home, we didn't feel welcome or wanted anywhere. We were the new kids on the block and the newest entrants in established classes at school. School, home, and the neighborhood were our world; we did little outside of them and had no friends our age beyond them. In fact, at double my age, Jannie was our main playmate; there were so few in the neighborhood. Put lightly, it was an undesirable situation, all around.

After we'd been in Phoenix a while our real mother decided to fly in to see us. We were so excited we could hardly wait. My feet just danced up and down in anticipation, and I chattered about it constantly, which I am sure didn't give my stepmother any warm, fuzzy feelings. Finally the day arrived. It was in the middle of May and already very hot. The dry desert air is different from the humid heat of Florida. Unfortunately, Mother stepped off the plane, took in a deep breath, and keeled over in a dead faint. She took a taxi to the house but had already made up her mind to go back home immediately. She said her head hurt from striking it when she fell. We only got to spend about three hours with her. I showed her all around the house. I showed her Baby Dolly and told how I helped take care of her. I showed her where Joy and I slept together and where Ray slept. She even held Ray on her lap a minute. Then she called a taxicab and left. She'd planned to stay three days but "just couldn't," she said. She never came back. Once again, I felt bereft and totally abandoned. Much later I learned that she had stayed in a fancy Phoenix hotel for three days after she left us, but she never called to let us know she was still in town. Although I only learned that much later, the pain was fresh upon learning how little she cared. It is still a fresh feeling, decades later.

After Joy and Ray and I had been in Arizona a short while with our new family, I began having stomach pains that got worse and worse as the days passed. I would roll on the bed in pain, until finally, after some questioning, my parents learned that I hadn't had a bowel movement in two weeks. An appointment was finally made to take me to a doctor. It was the first time I had ever had a medical appointment or seen a physician.

The day arrived. By then I had been filled with stories by Jannie until I was terrified. Even though they did not have appointments, Joy and Ray had to go with us since they were not in school. My feet grew heavier as we walked toward the doctor's office, and my stomach began corkscrew twistings and labyrinthine turnings. We were in the waiting room trying to sit quietly when suddenly I got sick and had to go to the bathroom immediately. I was so frightened my bowels turned to Jell-O, I guess; I had diarrhea! I told Stepmother when I returned to the waiting room and watched her scowl turn into a satisfied smirk. When my name was called she explained the situation and told the nurse that I was okay and wouldn't need to see the doctor after all. "Wait right here," the nurse said and entered the doctor's office. Earlier, as the doctor crossed the office moving from one room to another I noticed his eyes stop a moment on us as he glanced at each patient, but his searching look made no great impression on me. The nurse relayed Stepmother's message and returned with his reply. The doctor was a wise man who could see beyond present appearances, and his glance had taken in more than I realized. "I still want to see the patient," he told the nurse. I couldn't figure out why, since he had already seen me when he passed by once on his way to the office room. But no one told me why, and I was too terrified to ask. It took hours to cross the office waiting room and enter the office. Stepmother was pushing me in the door by the time we reached the threshold. I sat on a chair, feet dangling in the air, looking at one rumpled sock that had slithered down around my ankle. My eyes seemed too heavy to lift, but when I finally forced a glance I saw that he sat behind his desk, a long snake-shaped rubber thing around his neck, scowling more and more. Then he examined me. He chatted away, asking me questions and trying to get me to relax. The rubber snake was a stethoscope, he said. As the examination progressed he got quieter and quieter. After it was finished he seemed very angry. I didn't know why he was so mad until many years later, because I was sent back to the waiting room while he talked with Stepmother. I knew he'd also glimpsed Joy and Ray in the waiting room when he passed by that one time. Now he demanded to see them too. All three of us looked like waifs. We were all seriously malnourished. Joy and I were so thin and anemic he insisted on starting iron shots immediately. We had never had any childhood immunizations, so we had to have smallpox shots also. They hurt painfully. Our little arms were so small that our smallpox shots had to be given elsewhere. They decided on our backs toward the right side because the doctor said the skin was stretched until it was lying right against the bones of our arms. I still have the scar on my back where the shots were given. Just to exacerbate things, it seemed, he discovered that we also had infected tonsils.

Joy and I especially stayed sick a lot. Our throats were always sore. We didn't realize then that we were so malnourished that we had no resistance and were easy prey for strep throat and infected tonsils. The doctor decided to take both our tonsils and adenoids out. We were put into the hospital separately, me first. After the operation we each stayed a few hours and then went home. When I came to in recovery they were trying to coax me to eat vanilla ice cream, but I wasn't having it. I kept begging for mashed potatoes, but they said no. Finally they offered strawberry flavored ice cream and I accepted. After a few nosebleeds I went home. Then Joy's were removed the same way.

The hospital was a good experience in spite of the operation and the pain and the fright of an all-new environment. I think that was because everyone there seemed to care about me and my comfort. It was only for a few hours that I felt so treasured, but I wonder if that is one reason why I went into medicine when I was choosing a career. Like spilled syrup, a little love can spread a long way, leaving sweetness wherever it touches.

Our long period of illnesses was not over yet, however. The lady across the street, Mrs. Hurlbert, made Joy and me little matching sun dresses and Ray matching shorts out of a piece of fabric she had. The three of us were so proud! One day we went and sat out in the bright sun a while so passersby could see us. Then we came in, admiring our sudden "suntans." Later, a close inspection by adults showed that our "suntans" were really German measles, brought out by the sun. We were all sick, but my temperature soared the most. Finally Daddy decided that since my fever was so high and wouldn't go down, I must have worms. He went to the feed store and bought huge animal worm pills, which were shoved down my throat. My fever continued to climb. More horse pills. More fever. Finally in disgusted desperation a call was put out for the doctor, who still made house calls. When he arrived, he came in to the bedroom to check me out.

"I'm going to give you a little medicine," he said. I began to cry and begged him not to give me any more of those big horse pills.

"Girl, what are you talking about?" he demanded.

"The big horse pills; please don't make me take any more of them!"

He went out to the living room and asked my parents what I was talking about.

Daddy told him, "She wasn't getting better, so I figured she must have worms." I wasn't getting well because I was "wormy"?

"Let me see those pills."

The pills were brought forth, and the doctor exploded.

"What are you trying to do? Kill her?" He threatened Daddy and told him it might have killed me; those pills are meant for horses! Daddy admitted that he got them at the local feed store because it was cheaper than the drugstore. The doctor forbade Daddy to give us any more of those pills, and he didn't, but after that they never took any of us to the doctor again, except once. I think Daddy was a little afraid of him.

I finally got over the German measles, but the doctor was destined to be called in once more before Daddy quit letting us go to him. Before long I got chicken pox! Baby Dolly also got them. It was bad on Dolly as she was still only a baby. The doctor treated her, and then he decided to give Joy and me gamma globulin shots, hoping to stop our sicknesses. It seemed to help; I didn't have as many illnesses after that. Finally, our long period of sicknesses seemed to come to an end.

It was some months later that my hand got slammed in a car door. Daddy bandaged up the finger. That was that. The finger kept hurting, but I didn't dare complain. The bandage grew old and raggedy, with bloody streaks showing through. Then it turned sort of green, but still, I said nothing. I was afraid. Finally one day the teacher started complaining about the foul smell in the classroom. "What is that smell? It's terrible!" She stalked around the room, sniffing. When she neared my desk she hesitated and looked at me carefully. That's when she saw the bandage. "What in the world!" she exclaimed. "What is wrong with your finger?" I held the bloody green bandage up apologetically. I didn't know what I had done or hadn't done, but I knew that she wasn't pleased with me. "You go home and tell your parents to get you to a doctor! That finger has gangrene in it!"

I did as she said and repeated her words to Daddy.

"Hmmph. Thinks she can diagnose, does she? Well, you don't need no doctor; I can take care of that m'self. And it's infected, but not gangrenous."

Daddy put a pan of water on the stove. When it was steaming, he poured Clorox in it and called me over. "Give me your finger, girl. Let me see it now." He unwrapped the foul-smelling rags of red and slimy green and took my hand, and before I knew what he was doing, he had plunged the whole hand into the partially bubbling water. He held it there despite my screams and struggles. Perhaps he was right; at least we didn't have to go to the doctor. The skin sloughed off, the blisters broke, and the finger healed eventually. Later, even the scars of remembered pain faded some, although I still have the physical scars to this day. I never thought much about it after that, and I am sure Daddy didn't either. He was right because he was "always right" and because it saved him a visit to the doctor. He never liked doctors and always believed in home cures.

The effect of that unexpected deliberate pain on my psyche was something that he probably never gave a thought to, just like parents or mates today give little thought to their tone of voice or belittling remarks. Unaware, they are causing scars of lasting duration, all because they lack the sensitivity to see what they are doing. Is there a way to sensitize our words? Is it possible to stand back and look at our voices, tones of voices, words we say, and hear them with ears other than our own? Is it possible to cut out the cancer of thoughtless abuse? Abuse is abuse, intended or not. And no person is "always right."

My mother once sent me a book on Raggedy Ann and Andy that I still have, fifty years later. The book said that Raggedy Ann had a real heart in her little cotton body, so I made what I thought was a logical assumption and decided that all dolls had real hearts inside them. Following my surgery I had become fascinated with operations and so, a la Raggedy Ann, I began operating on my old rubber doll, cutting her up, looking for tonsils etc. She always died during surgery and I'd bury her and then later would resurrect her. She always came back to life. One day during her funeral I was called in to eat. It began to rain so I didn't get back out.

Consequently, I forgot about Betsy Wetsy's untimely demise. When I remembered, the mud had washed all signs of her gravesite away. After about three months, Daddy was digging a new septic tank and Betsy Wetsy's rotten little rubber body exited the ground. I was so upset!

Always before, Betsy's rubber body had come alive again and lived for another operation. This time she was so rotten that she crumbled in my hands. That's when I learned that stuffed dolls don't have hearts and rubber babies can't be resurrected, any more than broken childhood dreams can be repaired. The glue called love is the only thing that repairs those broken dreams, and even then, it is a lifelong process in many cases.

Chapter Nine

GRANDMA'S SUGAR BOWL

From the very first day we moved Jannie was there, hanging around the house. She and her two brothers—Eddie, six, and Ronnie, five—were the only children in the neighborhood to play with, so when she latched onto us I never questioned the idea of a thirteen-year-old hanging out with a five-year-old and a four-year-old. Lee was close to her age, so I guess that accounted for it. She hung around a lot, often slipping down to the woods with Lee and Gil. Lee had Old Missy as a pet and even had a horse of his own. I would have loved to have a pet, but our desires were invisible gossamer threads, unseen and undetected by the adults.

Gradually I made friends with Jannie, whose home became a sort of refuge to me. Autumn was slipping across the desert and into our yards the morning I decided to go to Jannie's. To get to her house you had to walk a path through our backyard and go through a big field into their yard. The dry grass sang a rustling melody of summer's end, which matched the trill in my heart. Using a new double skip I'd learned, I skipped over grassy clumps, filled with the anticipation of being with Jannie, her mother, and a visiting grandmother. As we sat in her house, her grandmother began showing me how to cut out a paper doll from a magazine picture. This was before Dolly was born, and as long as I didn't bother Stepmother I was allowed to go anywhere. However, I had to always go home if I needed to use the bathroom, because other people's bathrooms might "be nasty." Later I was to wonder if that rule was imposed to give Stepmother an occasional awareness of my whereabouts. Perhaps there was some concern for us buried within her after all. I will never know. After I had been there a while, I got up and obediently skipped back home to use the bathroom and then rushed back so as to not miss anything. No one seemed to be home at my house.

A while later, there was suddenly a hard banging at the door at Jannie's house. Her mother answered it. Our dog, Old Missy, had followed me into Jannie's house and was sitting patiently beside me. When Jannie's mother opened the door Old Missy suddenly jumped in front of me, teeth bared, growling horribly at my stepmother, who loomed there with a razor strap held firmly in her large hands. It was as if Old Missy sensed what was to come and was trying to protect me from it. Stepmother stalked inside and lunged for me, but Missy stood in front of me, growling. I had no idea why Stepmother was looming over me with a razor strap. I hadn't done anything that I knew of, but immediate terror began filling me to the brim of my frightened eyes. About then my stepmother told Jannie's mother to open the door to another room and lock Missy up. Reluctantly, she slowly opened the door. My stepmother put down the strap and ordered Missy to go into the room. With the strap relinquished, Old Missy obediently went, but as soon as the lock snapped behind her, there came growling and snarling again from behind the door.

Does evil clog the atmosphere with a pervasive smell we fail to recognize but dogs are aware of? At that moment Missy somehow knew more than I did.

"What in the world is that strap for?" Jannie's mother asked.

"That kid broke my mother's sugar bowl, and she's going to pay for it good!"

"Oh, no," Jannie's mother exclaimed. "She's been there with us all afternoon except for a short time when she insisted on going home to go to the bathroom."

Years later I realized that she was trying to defend and protect me without irrevocably offending Stepmother. Right then I was too full of terror to think logically about anything. At age six I was rapidly learning to be absolutely obedient, in hopes that it would lessen the beatings I received. What could I have done in the short time I was in the house, and why did she think I had broken her sugar bowl? I had no knowledge even of its existence. Later I learned that it had been packed away, high up in the cupboard. She kept sugar cubes in it and gave them to Lee and Gil for treats. Joy, Ray, and I never got treats, so I had no idea it was there. I didn't know what was wrong. Terror was suffocating me, clogging my nostrils, dropping dark sacks of black across my face, over my eyes and mouth.

"The other kids, Lee and Gil, saw her go into the house and told me, so she must be the one to have broken it," my stepmother snarled.

She grabbed me and dragged me backward by my two long pigtails all the way home, with me trying to run backward, screaming and crying, "I didn't do it!" as she alternately beat me with the strap and then pulled me behind her. I couldn't run backward, so I stumbled often. Each time I faltered, my head was yanked so hard it pulled me back up to run and fall again. The trip home was an agony of pulled hair, the strap randomly lacerating and lacing my body, tears of terror choking my breath.

My stepmother was a big woman, almost six feet tall and close to three hundred pounds. To her, slinging me around was like pulling a small chicken across the yard. Jannie's mother stood in the doorway and watched me being pulled home, hands up to her mouth, eyes wide in disbelief. But she didn't attempt to interfere again. She didn't dare. Furthermore, Jannie told me later that I was not to come back to her house to play because her grandmother, who had a heart condition, had nearly had a heart attack from that episode. Jannie said they couldn't take a chance with that happening again, so I was not to return. "But I didn't do anything," I protested. It didn't matter; I was not to return.

I was filled with terror, abandoned and bereft, and justice was a shadowy, hollow well in which hope slowly drowned. When we got home, Stepmother beat me with the razor strap until, once again, blood mixed with urine ran down my legs. Where she hit me on the shoulders and legs great welts raised up. Finally, exhausted, she stopped and literally threw me into a corner where my head hit the wall and I slid to the floor, barely conscious. I huddled where she'd thrown me, sobbing and choking yet trying not to cry or call attention to myself. "Sulking," she called it, any time I wept.

Jannie's mother released Old Missy about half an hour later. Missy really wasn't my dog; she belonged to Lee and Gil. My stepmother had had old Missy since she was a puppy. When she got home she began licking my face and legs, whining. Maybe they owned her, but she was my champion that day and I loved her forever after.

Soon after old Missy got back, Gil, my stepbrother who was six months younger than me, came home. He watched me in the corner for a while, listening to my hiccoughing sobs. Soon after, he climbed into his mother's lap, smiled sweetly, and kissed her. "Mommy, I'm sorry, but I broke your sugar bowl today. It was an accident, and I'm really, really sorry. I was just trying to get one of your delicious treats," he said as he curled up in her lap. His words were smooth honey sliding onto the platter of his mother's psyche.

After a moment's silence she said, "Son, I'm proud of you. Because you told me the truth you won't be punished."

I listened with unbelieving ears. By now I had lost the weight gained by staying at Grandma and Grandpa's. My weight was disgraceful; nevertheless, with all my undernourished twenty-three pounds of indignation, I said, "He broke it and I got beat for it and he gets nothing?"

With Tommy all curled up and cuddled in her lap, the sole center of her attention, Stepmother barely bothered to look toward my corner. As she glanced my way her narrowed eyes and tight mouth were like additional blows as she spat out, "Shut up, you poor little dumbbell. You'll forget all about it in a few years or so." Her bitter-hard look told me what an embarrassing and despicable object I was. Then even her unruly eyebrows seemed to soften and gentle as her face changed into a crooning smile and her head swung back to Gil. That was the end of it, for her.

My stepmother was wrong about one thing: I never forgot that injustice. Nor did I forget the terror and shame of being dragged backward across the yards, in full view of the neighbors. I will always remember the beating and the ooze of warm urine and blood inching down my legs at the house. No, I was never to forget the afternoon of the sugar bowl. It was a reminder that life was not fair and that I was better off if I didn't expect anything, for then I would never be disappointed. In a way, you might say it was the beginning of the end of childhood expectations. Justice had become a mockery and fairness a contemptuous wad of sodden longing choking my stuffed throat. My world had been savagely flattened. I learned that day that my inner earth had edges and endings from which a small child could easily be toppled.

If only she had said just two words—"I'm sorry"—how different my memories would have been and how different my understanding of justice might have become. There's so much power in those two little words!

Chapter Ten

THANKSGIVING TURKEY

Life was not always grim in those early days of my life. Occasionally some event ignited sparks of humor that would lighten my days. The salvation of humor has stuck with me from then until now. I often wonder if my humor began with that year on Grandma and Granddad Love's farm or if it was simply a genetic implant in me. However my ability to see humor in most situations came into being, it was a reality that rescued me from many an intolerable situation. As a six-year-old, for instance, funniness overcame fear whenever I thought of Thanksgiving dinner our first year in Phoenix.

We three had been in Phoenix less than six months when Thanksgiving rolled around. Grandma and Grandpa Bush, my stepmother's adoptive parents, came for dinner that year, so we were nine in all. It was a jolly day; odors emanated from the kitchen that made my stomach roll in delight and anticipation. I wore my best dress, which wasn't very best at all but was what I had. You learn early to "use it up, wear it out, make do, or do without" when driven by necessity.

Most of my things weren't really considered worn out until I had worn them out twice over and even the holes had holes.

Starlight was poking holes in the blanket of night before we sat down to Thanksgiving dinner. The nine of us gathered just under the ceiling light around a fat, golden turkey, roasted "to perfection." Mashed potatoes, my "most favorite" food in the entire world, formed snow-topped mountain peaks in the pretty blue bowl. Pumpkin pie stood on the sideboard, ready to sacrifice itself for the anticipated finale of our feast. Stepmother and Grandma Bush had outdone themselves;

the sights and smells blended into one glorious, to-be-remembered moment.

Our only light source was dull streaks of light emanating from a single ceiling bulb, which created chilly shadows and dark corners in the room. To be in the light was to be safe. I made sure I was as close to that light source as I could get. The shadows made me uneasy, as if something was about to happen.

I thought my stomach was growling awfully loud when I realized that it wasn't my stomach; it was a rumble from outdoors! We had seated ourselves, ready to eat, when a big storm rolled up from nowhere. Even over the clatter, chatter, and chewing of nine people it abraded our consciousness. The sky was a gigantic firefly, flickering against a backdrop of desert darkness, and thunder resounded like an ominous voice of God, deep-bellied and rolling. Daddy was preparing to carve the turkey, knife and fork in hand. He cleared his throat and flourished the implements in a moment of self-importance as he began to lean over the turkey. It was time to make that first careful cut. Without warning the storm attacked with sharp teeth of lightning and roars of anger. Daddy wasn't yet touching the turkey when we heard lightning snap against our roof. Instantly a bolt flashed down through the ceiling light, right into the turkey, singeing and charring it. There was a putrid smell of death and rot mixed with that ozone smell peculiar to lightning. Underlying it all was the neck-choking odor of burnt meat permeating the air.

"Get down! Get away from the table!" Daddy bellowed as he dropped to his knees. Immediately, all the lights spit out. We were left in smothering darkness, blanketed by the smell of charred turkey and ozone. Daddy crawled from the room, mumbling about finding a flashlight somewhere. Exactly where and why a flashlight would be on the floor is something I wondered about for a long time. At the time it made Daddy seem courageous and brave. Above us, shards of the useless single bulb hung like a crucifix from the ceiling.

Finally Daddy returned with candles and a flashlight and we regrouped around the table, the horrible smell of burnt turkey flesh hanging in the air. If perchance the turkey *had* been a little undercooked before, it was well done now. We had to eat the meat; Daddy insisted that it not be wasted. The taste was terrible. I didn't really mind; I still had my virgin white mashed potatoes. Burying the charred vestiges in a pile of potatoes and packing my white clouds all around the burned stumps meant that it could be swallowed more easily.

Sometimes the hand of God seems to touch us in strange ways. While I didn't think in such philosophical ways at age six I was aware enough to realize that had Daddy been touching that turkey with the knife and fork in his hands as he leaned over he would have been as charcoaled as the turkey. I wonder if he realized that his life had been spared. Did he experience relief or ask "why" or think about the purpose of his life? Probably not. Not my Daddy.

Regardless, I will never forget the holiday fireworks of my first Phoenix Thanksgiving when lightning cooked the turkey and Daddy became very human and very, very frightened for a few minutes. It was nice to know the adults who so rigidly controlled us had no control at all over the forces of nature, which could shake their day, singe their turkey, and leave them crawling about blindly in the dark, all dignity forfeited.

It was the day I began discovering my funny bone, which was to become a defense and a deflector. It gave me a needed objectivity and removed my mind from the pain that often pervaded my existence. Thank God for an ability to see humor in unlikely situations!

There were occasional years when humor invaded and alleviated painful experiences, but they were all too rare. Coming from Grandma and Grandpa's just months before, it was pure grace that allowed this Thanksgiving time to be one of them. It helped lessen the step-down displacement from grandparents to parents. There were not to be many more such times.

Chapter Eleven

A LITTER OF PUPPIES

Jannie, at thirteen, was more interested in sex than most of the rest of us were. At age five I knew absolutely nothing about sex and, like most of us young ones, could have cared less. One day she decided the new dumb little greenhorns needed a sex education. She had come to the house to ask us to play outside. Gil and Lee were already with her. When Joy and Ray and I got out we were forced to sit while she showed dirty pictures and "explained life," as she put it. We were told not to tell anyone what we had learned and threatened with dire consequences if we did.

Dark memories began to swirl around me in the ensuing days, making me uneasy and frightened. I was upset and unsettled because she said not to tell. It just didn't feel right. It frightened me. There were echoes of what Daddy did to me whenever he got a chance. He always said the same thing, saying, "Don't tell anyone," and threatening to "beat me to death" if I did. Why couldn't we ever tell anyone if these things were okay as he said they were?

One quiet late summer day Jannie came over. She'd seen an ad in the newspaper to sell puppies. She'd also seen a story about a monkey who mated with a cat and had babies, or so she said. Jannie, at thirteen, and Lee, twelve, were fascinated by the story. Jannie said that she was going to make a lot of money by mating a dog with a girl. She caught an old male dog that hung around and masturbated him until he started yelping and sprayed white semen into a cup she was holding under him while Lee and Gil held him. I didn't know what she was doing at the time and didn't understand the white stuff, but I never forgot the events of that fateful day.

She told us all to come with her. Autumn winds rustled the trees, showering us with early fall yellow leaves as we snaked our way around tall cottonwoods and some fallen trees. She took us to the wooded pasture on the back of their land where there was a tree that wasn't too tall. It had a sturdy branch growing out about five feet from the ground. Jannie threw a rope over the low-hanging branch and made a sort of lasso or hangman's noose. She and the boys had already made their plans.

Lee and Gil ran to me, grabbed my arms, and held me while she pulled my underpants off. She was so much bigger that kicking didn't help. Then they forced my foot through the loop in the noose and pulled me upside down so I hung by one ankle from the tree, screaming and crying, bracing myself with my hands against the ground. She told the other kids that she probably needed to add water to make more puppies as there "wasn't enough seaman in the cup." She acted so smart, like she knew what she was doing, measuring with an old measuring cup.

Soon, she was ready and the boys held me as she tried to pour mixture into me. I kicked and struggled for all I was worth, screaming all the while, but no one heard me. We were too far away from all the houses. She took one of the boy's belts and belted my other foot to the hanging ankle so I couldn't "force it all out by kicking." They left me hanging upside down like a piece of hanging meat to let it sink down inside me before they finally took me down. Jannie said we needed time to make sure it "took" and she'd have to check me every few days to see if it was pregnant. For days I was too terrified to go out to play. I kept hanging around playing with Dolly and working inside folding clothes and finding other work to do. I feared her knock at the door.

My ongoing sobs at night as I lay rigid in terror were of no comfort, for I was the only one who cared what had happened. What if I had puppies? No one to ask. No one to tell me.

Since I had previously thought Jannie was my friend, I had told her all about my real mother. Distance and present circumstances made Mother seem like an angel, and that's how I described her, I guess. I gave Jannie the ultimate weapon that time. Now she knew how to terrify me. She said that if I told anyone, she'd kill my real mother. My mother! I believed her, even though my real mother was in Florida and thirteen-year-old Jannie lived in Arizona. A thirteen-year-old to me was an adult. It seemed entirely possible that she could do this. Sometimes Jannie would take me to her old outhouse, light a cigarette, bend me over, and burn my butt with it, threatening to kill Mother if I told anyone about our activities. She knew how such threats about Mother terrorized me. She knew how much I loved my mother. At times I had so many cigarette blisters on my backside that I could barely sit. If that was the price I had to pay to keep my mother safe, it was worth it.

I never told anyone anything until the day Jannie came to my door to see if I was pregnant. She grabbed me and began to feel my stomach to see if I was getting bigger. I began screaming, crying, "I don't want to have puppies! Please don't make me have puppies." Stepmother heard me screaming and wanted to know what was going on, so I told her.

When Daddy came home that evening, she told him what I had, in my panic, told her; consequently the kids got chewed out. I heard Daddy tell Lee and Gil that there "had better not be any more such shenanigans." That was the sum total of their punishment for all my time of torment! They didn't get a whipping, and neither of them even had to apologize.

No one spoke to me about it at all. No one came to comfort me or try to alleviate my horror, pain, and fear. It was if the "incident" had never happened. That didn't stop them; they just didn't play with me anymore. It was after that that they all began to torment me.

We were told we had to be home at dusk. Sometimes when Ray and I walked across the darkening fields so full of grass and weeds, Jannie, Lee, and Gil would make ghost noises and then jump out at us. When I went home crying and told Stepmother what had happened, they'd all say they didn't do it.

Once the kids pushed me out of a high tree we were climbing, but fortunately I wasn't injured. If I told on them they denied it; consequently, I'd get the whipping for lying while Lee, Gil, and Jannie, the ringleaders, were only scolded.

A child begins life by believing that life is fair. Disillusionment sets in when peers get scolded while you get beaten when you were innocent, or at worst, when they were equal participants in the misdemeanor. Life's experiences were crumbling my conceived walls of justice. Little did I know that those walls would soon be blasted away, leaving a rubble of innocence.

Eventually I was allowed back in their good graces long enough to play at a mock wedding. Jannie and some of the others were all playing "wedding." The boys took gunny sacks, and the girls put them on their heads for veils and made baling-wire wedding rings. Jannie's brother, seven-year-old Eddie, was chosen to "marry" me, but he said he wouldn't because "her nose is always running." The rejection cut deep because secretly I felt like a faulty faucet anyway; I always had a cold or strep throat. I was so malnourished that I had no reserves to fight colds, disease, or infection. Eddie told me to go home and wipe my nose and gave me a rough shove to indicate that I should be moving. I stumbled off feeling like a runny egg that had been dropped and stepped on.

When I got home, Baby Dolly was awake from her nap, so I played with her for a while, still feeling hurt and angry from Eddie's remarks. Suddenly I had a flash of inspiration too great to be resisted. The impulse prodded me up to my feet and out the door. There temptation became an irresistible magnet, drawing me to the barn.

My father had long been a skilled hand at finding bargains. One of his regular places was the bakery. He would buy outdated foods from the bakery and use the contents to feed the pigs and even the cow.

Hay motes danced in the dusty air. Summer-sweet smells emanated from the scratchy bales of hay stacked high in the barn, and sunshine slipped through the board cracks, turning the world into a striped fantasy of fragrant quietness. Again that ineluctable magnetism gripped and propelled me toward an empty stall. I knew right where to go.

There was the big old burlap bag of Daddy's, bulging with stale bread, old cookies, dry pies, and cakes. Reaching as far as a little girl's skinny arm would go I groped for a cookie from the "old foods" bag. Back then old meant old, and the dryness of the old food should have removed all temptation, but I ate them all the time.

When you are hungry you will eat anything. Sometimes I even ate the mesquite beans in the yard. Joy, Ray, and I were seriously malnourished during those years.

My searching fingers found the round hardness they were seeking in the bag, and I sped outdoors to the so-called pasture. A child bent on devilment can usually find a way to bedevil, so it wasn't long before my searching eyes located the object of its search. Lying nearby was a steamy, soggy, loose cow "pie," as we called the cow's droppings.

My search was ended; my mischief was about to begin. I opened that cookie up, bent over, and let it draw nearer and nearer to the cow pie. Each little descent brought cookie and cow pie closer, until the pie rubbed the cream side of cookie. When it was good and sticky, I closed the cookie up and went searching for Eddie. When I found him I skipped over and said to him,

"Eddie, I'm sorry I was mad at you for not marrying me when my nose was running. I've brought you a present to make up for it." Eddie snatched the cookie from my hand, popped the whole thing in his mouth as was his custom, and swallowed. After he was finished, I told him what I'd done. The kids began yelling, and Eddie hit me in the nose so hard my nose bled. Then he started screaming and trying to throw up. Jannie went running to my house and told my stepmother what I'd done. She, in turn, promised me a beating when Daddy got home, and sure enough, I got one. Daddy said I could have given Eddie worms and beat me even harder just talking about it. I wonder if Daddy ever had worms and if he had to take horse medicine. Was that what gave him such a dread of worms?

That was the only time in my entire childhood I ever sought revenge. I paid dearly for it; nevertheless, I felt gleeful over what I had done. I still chuckle now as I recollect it. I have often wondered where a little five-year-old "fraidy cat" got such an innovative idea, and the courage to implement it. There was that salvational humor again, cropping up in my life!

Not long after that, Jannie called us all together for another game of "mock wedding."

I was so naïve and innocent and dumb that the thought never occurred to me that they might have something cooked up especially for me … but they did.

"This time one of our wedding partners will be called on to consummate their union. That will be you, Jeanne," Jannie grinned.

"*Me!*? Why would I want to be constipated? I already am constipated." I retorted.

While I was still protesting, some of the children approached, threw me down on the ground, and held me there while one of the older boys "consummated" the marriage as my captors looked on. He was mature enough to be able to penetrate me. The episode didn't stop until I began projectile-vomiting and threw up in his face and on his shoulder. They let me go then.

The memory of that rape, which I not only never talked about but totally blocked out of my memory, was to remain buried under blankets of forgetfulness until over forty years later when intensive therapy brought it back in all its terror and shame.

After the "consummation," Jannie, Lee, and Gil said I was a tattletale and they didn't let me play with them. Even though I never told anyone, I went home that night sobbing brokenheartedly. My body was in pain and felt as though it had been pummeled. But worse, I knew that something very bad had happened to me and there was no one I could go to and tell. No one in my entire world I could go to for help. No one. Not one. What a sad echo to peal inside a child's head! Never had I felt so alone.

The kids still took Joy with them, who tried to act tough to win their approval, and Ray, who watched all mutely. I'd watch them walk off, headed into the woods to play, but to me, being shunned was a big favor. I was always relieved to see the backs of their heads.

The two adults in my little world, Stepmother and Daddy, would have denied that I had been raped, I suppose, but the aftereffects of that day dug scars as deep and dark as any grave. I buried my innocence in the twin graves of horror and memory on the day Jannie illustrated sex to us. Once lost, innocence can never be resurrected. Innocence is among the most mercurial and frangible qualities of life.

I felt as much a part of this family as a snowflake would living in deepest Africa. This family environment was my enemy and not supportive of my life. I was doomed to perish in this environment if I was there for very long.

Chapter Twelve

BIG JEAN'S BACKGROUND

Everyone has a story to tell. Each of us has reasons for being what we are. My stepmother was no different. I've learned that knowing the background of people is one way of approaching an understanding of them. With understanding, we can often come to forgiveness. *In order to destroy the power of a wrong, we must forgive it.*

Jean was born during the Depression, the fifth child born to a couple hard hit by the Depression. Her father had just lost his job, and they already had four kids. They felt that it would be better to give up the new baby than to give up one of the older ones, so after birth she was given to an orphanage to be put up for adoption. Imagine being given away because your parents didn't want you enough to struggle to keep you! Jean didn't remember being given up, of course, but the knowledge, gained later, affected the entire course of her life.

At nine months of age orphanage workers put her into a crib with another bigger child. The older child was stepping around in the crib when she broke little Jean's leg. Jean was in a full leg cast for a long time, healing slowly and enduring pain, left alone in a mostly untended crib. The event, consciously forgotten but known from records, almost surely scarred her subconsciously.

When she was finally adopted she was no longer an infant but an older child—an "orphanage brat." Grandma and Grandpa Bush, who had one son, my Uncle Dick, adopted her. Grandma couldn't have any more children because she was frail and sickly, weak. They decided to adopt a girl-child to help Grandma in the house. Grandma and Grandpa Bush lived in Phoenix, Arizona, at the time, but Grandma had a sister in Missouri named Alice. She was the key to Stepmother's future.

Aunt Alice, an RN, was married to an anesthesiologist. In our eyes, Aunt Alice and Uncle Jack had to be rich; they had a big three-story house. Because Uncle Jack was a doctor and Aunt Alice a nurse, it was easy for them to check confidential records at orphanages. It was decided that Aunt Alice would pick out a sturdy female with a strong resistance to illness. Big Jean was chosen. From her family's records she would be big-boned, strong, and tall, all of which she grew to be. When I knew her as my stepmother she was a woman about five foot eleven, very big-boned and weighing about 280 pounds.

When Aunt Alice and Uncle Jack took her to Grandma and Grandpa Bush's she met Uncle Dick, a thin, pale boy. He was also diabetic, which probably accounted for his frail, slender body. In that household, Uncle Dick could do no wrong, and perhaps that is where my stepmother got her twisted ideas of favoritism. Maybe she didn't know any other way, or perhaps, knowing that she was adopted, she felt less wanted. There was some basis for her perceptions, however, because Uncle Dick tormented her with all the glee of an older brother—a mean older brother.

When they were little, Uncle Dick would lure my stepmother to the basement to play, even though he knew full well that they weren't allowed in the basement. Because she wanted to please him, she always went. Once they were there, he'd run upstairs, leaving her behind and screaming, "Mom, Jean's playing in the basement again." She always got a whipping. She said she never learned. I think she did. I think those were her first lessons in Cruelty 101. She learned them well.

During the Depression another trick Uncle Dick sometimes played with her was when he would get a tin cup like ones used by street beggars. He would then lead my stepmother down the street, saying, "Money for the blind, money for the blind," while she staggered around like she couldn't see. When neighbors saw and reported them, they'd both get a whipping. Dick's was very light, but apparently Jean's was severe enough that she never forgot them. Is that where her ideas of severe, unfair punishment came from? Perhaps.

When he grew up, Uncle Dick married a Mexican woman who bore him our cousin Warren. Even after Uncle Dick became very ill and was a resident at the tuberculosis sanitarium, unable to live conjugally, she somehow continued to bear him numerous children from assorted donors. In fact, even after Uncle Dick was dead she continued to bear many children—in his honor, we presumed. After he was discharged from the sanitarium, Uncle Dick returned home to live with Grandma and Grandpa Bush. Little Warren came with him. His wife continued to spend a lot of time bar-hopping but by then had deserted both Uncle Dick and Warren so no longer played a part in their lives except as a dying ember in a long-forgotten fire. Warren continued to live with my Uncle Dick and later with Granddad Bush.

Grandpa Bush worked for the gas company and was one of the lucky ones who never lost his job during the Depression. He used to tell how once on the day before Christmas he was ordered to shut off a family's gas. When he got there, the mother begged him to give her a little more time; she was cooking the children's Christmas dinner. Her little scrawny children all were staring at him. He wasn't supposed to do this, but it was Christmas and he figured that no one would know, so he said he had another job to do first. He turned away from their hungry stares and went on. When he got back she was still using the oven, but he told her he just had to turn it off. She opened her old stove oven and pulled out a roaster pan with the only Christmas dinner she could offer her children—five little puppies. They'd been skinned, but you could still tell by looking what they were. After he reluctantly turned off the gas, Granddad went outside and threw up. Jean never forgot that story. Neither did I, when I heard it years later. Hunger takes many forms. So does a hunger for love.

Years passed. Jean was expected to help Grandma Bush and to always be there for her. She knew, of course, that she was adopted. Now she knew why. Her parents hadn't wanted her, and the Bushes needed her youth and strength. As far as we knew, she was never deeply abused, but she always felt unloved or second best or appreciated only for what she could give rather than who she was. Eventually she grew up and married Strong, a strong-jawed, good-looking young policeman. At first things were lovely, but then theirs became a volatile relationship. They fought all the time.

One day a bill came to the house for a dozen roses with a card for Teresa. That was how Big Jean learned that Strong was running out on her with another woman. Jean waited for Strong to come home. She'd heated leftover spaghetti for lunch, which he didn't like. She knew what his reaction would be. Sure enough, Strong began yelling that he wouldn't eat that pig slop; it was "no good the first time and he wasn't eating it a second time." Finally, voice-tired and spirit-weary, he went to bed to take a nap. While he slept she grabbed the bowl of spaghetti and ran outside to their old car. Still angry, she dumped the bowl of spaghetti on the windshield, smeared blood-red sauce and white, wormy strings of spaghetti all over, and turned the wipers on to spread it good. Her sense of satisfied vindictiveness faded, however, when it turned out that she needed to use the car first. She did have a sense of humor, which is why we heard the story as kids. Trouble is, we rarely saw that side of her.

Together Strong and Jean had two little boys, Lee and Gil. It was not enough to hold the marriage together, however. When they got divorced Jean got custody of Lee and Gil and Strong married his Teresa, a beautiful, strong-willed woman whose parents came over from Sicily. Her parents set her up with a grocery store. The grocery store prospered while Strong enjoyed promotions as a policeman. Together they had three kids: Rosalie, Charlie, and Patty. Strong built onto their house and really made it nice. In years to come he dug a big swimming pool with Lee and Gil and Charlie's help and built his girls, Rosalie and Patty, a big playhouse by the pool.

In those days bomb shelters were in. In school we were given drills for bombs. When the alarm sounded we had to fling ourselves onto the floor and under our desks, turtle style. So Strong dug a bomb shelter leading from the master bedroom in their house to under the store on the lot next door. One day, the boys opened up the door into the bomb shelter and took us down underneath, down the long dark tunnel under the house, and into next door under the store. There on shelves along the wall were foodstuffs for emergencies. There was bedding and all the things you needed in a bomb shelter.

What the kids had to show us, however, was in a glass jar. In it was the cut-off thumb of a "Jane Doe," an accident victim. She'd been hit by a car and never identified. Her thumb had been kept for possible future identification. Knowing I was the "fraidy cat," the kids put the jar in my hand and told me not to drop it or the thumb would come alive. The thumb was preserved in a clear solution but had already acquired a greenish cast. Then they turned the light out on me. The kids listened as I screamed and cried for help, until Strong came down and ran us all out. How they all laughed at the joke they had played. All but me, that is. I had nightmares for weeks after.

All along, Strong had been paying child support for Lee and Gil. I was not really to know him until he became my "defender" at the motel, but even before that, when I learned how he worked and built for his family, he became a hero to me. I tried to imagine what it must be like to have a dad who would build a swimming pool or a playhouse for you and who had the money to do such things; a dad who didn't move every few months and who was consistent in personality and affections. A father who didn't beat you or scare you with the things he did to you. A good man whose hands didn't give you nightmares of being groped. I could imagine it only because I had seen it in Strong. That's when I first realized that all fathers are not the same.

After Strong and Jean's divorce, she went to work at the Java Café in Phoenix, where she met our daddy. She had custody of Lee and Gil. Whenever we all went to Strong and Teresa's house for visitation times, they and their three children always treated us very well. In fact, after Daddy and Jean sold the house on Orange Road, they let us move into one of the rental motel apartments behind their house for a while, before Daddy moved us to Missouri. That was when Strong really became my hero and my rescuer.

In years to come, Strong and Teresa bought properties to rent out. They prospered in every way but never got "too grand" for us. I loved the water, and Strong and Teresa let us play in their pool. One day Teresa and big Jean were sitting on the sides watching all the kids play. I had a little inner tube toy around me because I didn't know how to swim. It was wonderful, and I decided that I was a real water baby. One of the big kids dove in right beside me and somehow in their splash turned me and my inner tube upside down. I was so little and skinny I couldn't turn myself back over, and I couldn't get out. I was trapped, head and arms underwater, fighting to turn upright. Finally blackness began to cover me. I'd stopped kicking and struggling. Teresa noticed my still limp legs and swam over, grabbed me, and uprighted me. After I came to vomiting and spitting water, I didn't want to go near the water for a long time. I had nearly drowned. It was another event that burned deep into my memory. I never forgot that time of terror. It wasn't even the terror that bothered me so much; it was the fact that terror was becoming a common factor in my days, or so it seemed. It was a trail of sticky slime that I could only follow and never escape. I was a slug trapped in the slime of my own trail of terror, and it felt like drowning: over my head, can't escape, can't breathe, trapped.

Chapter Thirteen

GRANDMA BUSH

The first years we were in Arizona I was left to take care of Grandma Bush just as Stepmother once did. She had congestive heart failure and pneumonia. Uncle Dick must have been in a nursing home then because of his TB and diabetes even though he was still fairly young. My last memory of him was of an extremely weak, small man in blue striped pajamas that accentuated his wonderful blue eyes. Uncle Dick earned small amounts of money by tatting exquisite lace and did beautiful embroidery, as did Grandma. Following Dick's divorce from the Mexican woman, Grandma and Grandpa had taken Warren to raise, but Grandma became ill and Warren was returned to his mother, leaving Grandmother alone during the day. This was where we entered the scene. I was six at the time and was left at Grandma's to take care of her while Grandpa went to work. She was not a well woman.

Grandma told me step by step what to do to help her, and after a few days I seemed to get the idea. I would shop for her too. Once I went to the store to buy her a jar of pickles, and I fell down while carrying them to the counter. The jar broke, and the pickles spilled all over the wooden floor. Would the owner beat me? How much? I was terrified as I watched his huge shoes approach and stop in front of me. He seemed taller than the sky, and his figure menaced me as he began to lean over. I was too frightened to move. He picked me up, dusted me off, and told me to get another jar. Then he took money for just one jar of pickles and sent me home. I never forgot that, for I expected to be badly beaten. I didn't know at that time that beatings were uncommon in the lives of most others. He probably soon dismissed it from his memory, but I never forgot that act of kindness. We never know how little kindnesses can live on in someone else's life.

One morning Grandma wanted me to cook oatmeal, but I couldn't light the old gas stove. I struck match after long wooden match across its rough surface only to have each go out. Grandma got off the old brown leather "fainting couch" and came to the kitchen to show me how, huffing and puffing all the way. Suddenly she fell into a chair and said, "Go call the neighbors to help," in a strange strangled voice. Frightened, I flew to the house of the woman closest to Grandma's. Somehow I knew with foreboding that life again was about to change.

The neighbor was a young woman with a baby. She hurriedly told me to watch the baby till she came back. I still remember that the baby was dressed in a yellow butterfly sunsuit that day.

Her apartment was just across the field from Grandma's, but proximity was all they shared in common. Her rooms were light and airy compared to Grandma's darkened house where the shades were always drawn to avoid "fading the drapes and rugs," as Grandma said. It kept the merciless Arizona sun out in the summertime. The neighbor's furniture, too, differed from the dark heavy furniture of the Bushes, and even the pictures were lighter, brighter. It was more than decoration; it was a declaration, declaring a philosophy of life.

In a short while, I heard ominous sounds filling the air, sounds I had heard many times in Phoenix. The baby and I watched as an ambulance pulled up at Grandma's front door. After they left, the young woman returned and said that I was to stay with her and the baby until Daddy got off work and could come for me. It had been early morning when Grandma couldn't breathe. She had been sleeping sitting up for nights, which meant nothing to my eight-year-old mind. Later we learned that she had pneumonia and congestive heart failure. All day I played with the baby and helped the lady fold clothes. At lunchtime she showed me how to make "tuna salad" sandwiches for lunch. I thought that was so wonderful! I didn't worry about Grandma because the neighbor said she was being taken care of at the hospital. Therefore the day was joyous in its newfandanglements.

When Daddy came that evening he greeted me with "You must not have taken very good care of Grandma if she had to go to the hospital!" Immediately and instantly afraid I was going to get a whipping, I began to cry. The neighbor lady asked Daddy to step outside; she'd like to speak to him. I heard her tell him I was far too young to have the kind of responsibility I'd been saddled with. She told him how I'd helped her all day long and how polite and obedient I was. She said quite a bit more. When she finished, Daddy came in and asked me if I was ready to go home. He was different on the way home. He was nice to me and even told me what the lady had said. The niceness didn't last very long, however.

Before her pneumonia and heart failure, while Grandma felt better she began trying to teach me to crochet and plain stitch on hankies. She would answer my questions, talk to me, and tell me about the books they had that she thought I'd like. *Five Little Peppers and How They Grew* was a special favorite of hers. Grandma Bush was nice company, and I was growing to not only love her but to trust her. She would not live much longer, however, and with her death my life once again shifted.

When Grandma died, her mass was held at a huge cathedral built of stone. The choir sang from the balcony while the priest and little altar boys walked up long aisles. Candles were lit, and their radiance in the twilight was magnificent in my eight-year-old eyes. I felt sad for my stepmother's tears, but I didn't truly realize that Grandma was gone for good. The choir sang "Ave Maria," and I felt goose bumps spreading across my arms and neck. To this day I still get them when I hear "Ave Maria." For a brief but unforgettable while I moved in a candlelit world of bright pinpointed effulgence, high notes of heavenly song, incense, and chants: a world of enchantment.

The Catholic mass is a beautiful ceremony, but the woman in the casket bore no resemblance to Grandma. The finger-waved hair, powdered face, and plump rouged cheeks didn't look like her at all. She wore a tiny brooch at the neckline. My stepmother said they stuffed her cheeks with cotton to make her look healthy again.

Hers was my first experience with death. When our former baby-sitter held me over a casket trying to frighten me into behaving as she wanted, I had not associated it with death, but rather only with beatings. Until Grandma died, I had no concept, no real experience, with death. Grandma Bush's death was not frightening, only strange. It was a mixture of awe, sorrow, mystery, and beauty, like a variegated field of wildflowers that give infinite variety to the grasses beneath, wildflowers mixed with a wild grade of hay make for variegated bales of straw. Straw, used to soak up cattle dung, was also used to bed Baby Jesus. Dung or divinity: we can make of the straw what we will. The same was true of death, as I would learn much later when I viewed the lifeless bodies of two sons. We can wallow in the dung of death or clasp its divinity. The choice is ours.

Chapter Fourteen

MOTEL MOVE

Several months before Christmas came we were no longer on Orange Road. My footloose father, who always saw the pot of gold somewhere ahead, had decided to move us to Missouri. It was while we were still in Arizona, waiting to go to Missouri, that the episode of the blue pearl elephant necklace began. It would be played out to its bitter end after we moved to Missouri.

I yearned so deeply for the necklace and tried so hard those last six months before Christmas to be totally good; I just was certain that Santa would see and answer my deepest wish. It was then that the miserable Christmas I remember took place that told me how unloved I was. Joy deliberately got the gift I had longed for. It was like a rejection letter, signed by my stepmother, hammered by nails of disdain into my heart, telling me that I was truly and totally unloved. I turned away from everyone at that time and just lived somewhere inside myself like a motherless cub hibernating in an empty cave. I was the only person I could trust.

This was also the time when I learned that I should never ask for help in school. I'm terrible at math—always have been and always will be, because fear of math was beaten into me at this time by my father.

I was in the third grade, and math was coming hard. My stepmother always called me "the dummy," and I believed her. I considered myself stupid until, in my early fifties, my best friend began pointing out that my children were exceptionally intelligent and, being that they were half brothers and sisters how did I explain it? She began pointing out to me ways in which I excelled and characteristics that I had that denoted a high IQ. Finally I began to believe that maybe I wasn't stupid after all.

When I was struggling with math in the third grade, however, I was absolutely convinced that I was not "slow" but stupid. Believing in your own stupidity makes it harder to learn, and when you're afraid you won't get it, you don't.

When math became a problem, I went to my father for help. He explained it once or twice, but when my fear of being thought stupid kept me from grasping the concept, he'd grab me by the arm, yell the answer in my ear, and then beat me with the razor strap. Since he didn't do it every time I asked for help, I never knew when I would suddenly have my arm yanked and a strap applied to my legs and back. I didn't learn math very well, but I learned one other lesson exceptionally well: *don't ask for help.*

One night he beat me so hard that they could hear my screams and his curses all over the motel area. But those screams of pain and terror provided me with a defender. Strong, Lee and Gil's dad and the owner of the motel, came to our door and told my father that he couldn't make so much noise; adjacent customers were complaining. It was then, when he saw the condition I was in, that he realized what was going on. His face got red and ugly when he saw the strap marks on me, and right in front of us all he told my father never to lay a hand on me again or he'd answer to him for it! Daddy never did either, as long as we were at the motel. Of course, the beatings resumed harder than ever once we left there, but meantime, for a while, I had a defender. What sweet knowledge that was!

During this time my stepmother continued with the Machiavellian machinations of verbal abuse she had begun on Orange Road. She kept telling me how stupid I was and that I was "uglier than sin." If I heard how ugly I was once I heard it a zillion times. It still echoes in the caverns of my self-assessments, rippling on in endless sound waves.

Since I already was so self-conscious of my ears and my freckles and the wrong color of my eyes and my ugly-colored hair, it didn't take much to convince me that I must be the homeliest girl on earth. Again, it wasn't until I was much, much older that I realized that other people thought I was pretty! That, too, was hard to believe; to really inwardly accept in my room of self-opinion, where I lived. There had been too many years of being told how ugly I was for me to easily believe otherwise.

With some people this form of abuse is unconscious and not deliberate. They don't see themselves as abusers. They call it teasing or jesting or kidding, but it still is a form of abusing someone's self-esteem and sense of self-worth. Of all the varieties of abuse, verbal can be the very worst to the emotions and self-concepts we carry around. Unfortunately, my stepmother's remarks were not unconscious; they were deliberately destructive of esteem and confidence. They were invisible stones and unseen knives, pounding and lacerating me daily in the tenderest of places; my sense of self.

We went to school for three months while we lived in the motel. During that time our class was going to have a play. Most parts were already assigned, and I hadn't been picked for anything. One day the teacher said, "Now we are going to select the queen. How many of you have never been in a play?" Another new girl and I were the only two to raise our hands. The other girl was newer even than I was, and she was an attractive blonde with pretty blue eyes, curly hair, and a lovely, heart-shaped face. I waited for her name to be called, knowing that I was so ugly no one would choose me. Suddenly the boy next to me poked me in the ribs, hissing, "The teacher is calling your name!" Indeed she was. The teacher chose me! I couldn't believe it at first, and when I did I was so excited I thought I would float away and they'd have to pick someone else for their queen.

When school was out I flew home to tell the family. No one seemed to care much, but that didn't weaken my enthusiasm. I practiced and practiced my part until it was letter perfect. Finally the day of the play came. I tried to fix myself up as well as I could that day. My stepmother didn't comb or braid my long hair for the play, so I braided it myself. Nothing could dim my happiness that day, however, for I was a queen and I wore a beautiful gold crown so everyone would know I was the queen!

Neither of my parents came to the play, although all the other kids' mothers seemed to be there and some of the fathers as well. The only thing my parents ever attended during my school years was my graduation, because it was also Gil's graduation day. I happened to be in his class even though there was six months' difference in our ages.

It was the most beautiful play ever, I thought as I walked back to class afterward, with my gold crown still on. There was even a smile on my face, and suddenly I felt the smallest of flutters in my heart as if the hibernating cub was struggling to waken and emerge again. I think it must have been called hope. I suddenly found that I *could* hope again. I was hoping that my new classmates would accept me. Hoping that Daddy and Stepmother would see that I wasn't so ugly now and maybe like me a little. Hoping that maybe I'd grow out of being stupid and repulsive. Hoping that others would see something good in me; some sort of potential—for anything. It didn't matter what.

As I floated along the locker-lined hall an inch or two above the wooden well-oiled floor, a boy ran by and yanked my pigtail. "You are the ugliest thing I ever saw!" he shouted. My reverie of hope was broken like a balloon simultaneously punctured by a thousand darts. I began to cry. Ruth Ann Warren, one of the girls who had heard what they boy shouted, came over and, seeking to comfort me, said soothingly, "Don't you cry, Jeanne. My mother told me that anyone as ugly as you has to look better when they grow up." Ruth Ann was a nice girl, and I knew her words were meant to comfort me.

I liked Ruth Ann. I also remember envying her. One of her jumpers had grown too short, so her mother added bias tape and then embroidered pretty little ducks on the hem to give her additional use from the garment. I loved that jumper because the tape with hand-embroidered ducks showed such love for the little girl who wore it. To Ruth Ann, adults were kind people who loved you and always told the truth. I understand all that. But I didn't believe it anymore. I knew better than to believe that someday I would be prettier.

It was then that I realized why the teacher had chosen me. It was because she knew that I probably would never get chosen for any play again. I was too ugly. Ugly, ugly, *ugly!* It was something else I learned to carry through my days, like the echo of a falling stone bouncing emptily in my cave of broken hopes.

"Stupid and ugly": these words were to trail me down the path of my years in haunting reverberations. Stupid! Ugly!

We allow our perceptions to color our entire lives, neither questioning not taking into account the perceptions of others.

Chapter Fifteen

THE BLUE PEARL NECKLACE

It was love at first sight. It was the summer of my eighth birthday, and we were still in Arizona, preparing to move to Missouri. I was eight years old and was becoming aware of the adult world, in which one's dress and looks were important. We were preparing for a birthday party, and the night before it was to occur, my stepmother got the gift out to show us before it was wrapped.

Snuggled down in the box was a perfect set: a blue pearl elephant necklace and bracelet. Its lustrous baby-blue colors were the shade of a rich summer sky. It seemed to pull the light into itself, digest it, and then return it to the eye of the beholder in rich lambency. In that instant my world fell in an adoring heap before that wonderful gift. It immediately became the center of all my desires. "Oh, Mother," I begged, "please let me have that and we can get Jennifer another one. Please, Mother! I want it more than anything else in the whole world!" I bent over, hands clasped, begging Stepmother to let me have it. I cried and pleaded and told her I would stay home and not go to the party if she would let me have it. "If you let me have it, I'll find something else for Jennifer," I promised. Of course, I had no money to buy anything, and Stepmother knew this.

"There's another set down at Teresa's store. If you're really good, maybe Santa will bring it to you for Christmas!" she said with a strange smile. With that I had to be content. The set went to the birthday girl without the possibility of further discussion. Its rich blue colors were like the deep blue of Mother's eyes, the eyes Joy and Ray had but that I, so covetous, had failed to get. Perhaps I craved the set so much because it reminded me of the mother I never saw long enough, who never hugged us enough, never nurtured us sufficiently.

"I'd like that more than anything in the world," I confided to stepmother.

Never before had I expressed a desire to her for anything. This time my excitement overrode my silence. My desire had an almost tangible form. It was a bright, firm, and unchanging stone sinking into the softness of myself. My words were unexpected and spontaneous. Once more she reminded me, "If you're good, Santa may bring it to you for Christmas. But if you keep dinging about it you won't get anything."

We would be in Missouri before Christmas arrived. It was six months away. To the young, time is infinitely endless, stretching down a long corridor like an endless unwinding roll of ribbon. Six months was forever, but I knew better than to beg for it now. "Oh, I want it so much! I'll try real hard to be as good as I can, from now on!" I hoped my eyes looked as promising and pleading as I felt.

The night before the birthday party I could think of nothing but the necklace and bracelet. My heart centered on the baby-blue pearl pieces as if they were the sun rotating around the center of the universe. The next day, the first chance I got after school was out, I rushed down to the grocery. The blue pearl set was gone! Stepmother must have bought it! My heart was like a child's balsam toy glider, lofting higher and higher with each expectant wind. Those winds of expectation were to carry me through the next half year. Oh, I tried so hard, and I *was* good! As weeks crawled into months I hardly thought of anything else. If I had the blue necklace, it would be like carrying a piece of my mother around with me. If I could wear it, perhaps people would look at its beautiful blue and not notice my freckles, my jug-handle ears, or my lank stringy hair, which was forever getting snarled unless I wore it in pigtails. I quit talking and started working in order to deserve my pearl set.

In those six months I did everything I could think of to help my stepmother move and get settled in our new place as well as continuing my usual chores, and extra ones too. I did dishes and made beds, of course, but I also watched Dolly, folded clothes, emptied trash, and threw myself into any additional work I could find. I was certain that she would notice how good I was and how much I was helping. I didn't "ding" either, because I knew that if I did she'd have an excuse to not get the gift for me.

Hope is a sweet taste in the mouth, a huge bundle wrapped in brightly colored ribbons of expectations, a lighthouse in the sweeping darkness, and a bounce in the halls of the heart. Until it is fulfilled it remains what one might call a "hangnail in heaven." It hangs expectantly, hoping to be cut loose from its celestial mooring to be gently placed on the shores of reality. I just knew I would be getting my heart's desire that Christmas and the blue pearl necklace set would be mine.

On Christmas Eve morning I woke early. Knowing I'd be punished if I woke anyone else, I lay there watching a distant Missouri sun creep weakly toward the single window in our dwelling until it finally reached out to fill its entirety. The day had begun, and tonight we would open our gifts!

Throughout the day snow sprinkled gently across our Missouri world, each flake spearing itself on arrows of grass or smearing windows, cars, and buildings. Christmas carols strolled from the radio right into my soul, and I knew that this evening would be a birth of "most-wanted" happiness for me, just as Baby Jesus was Mary's "most-wanted."

We scrambled into the kitchen in the basement that evening after an incredibly slow-moving day. It was the only room that had any heat, and our sheet "walls" did prevent the stove's heat from entering, to a great degree. I'd heard the expression "slow as molasses," but that day was even slower. It moved by frozen millimeters like very cold molasses in subarctic weather.

In the basement no tree or crèche set proclaimed the greatest of births. There was no talk of a Christ child in that cramped little basement. Gifts were handed out, and mine was not yet among them. Everyone except Joy, Ray, and me had multiple gifts; for each of us there was only one gift. But I didn't care this time, because I knew. I just knew! Soon the blue gift would be mine! Finally Joy's name and mine were called out almost simultaneously. Joy tore the wrapping off hers, but I carefully undid stickers and paper, savoring my moment of certainty. Joy shrieked, "Look what I got!" and I glanced up as just as I was getting ready to lift the lid on my own box. Joy was holding her gift up for all to see. Impossibly, it was my blue pearl necklace and the bracelet.

I looked down at what I had received. There in the box lay a cheaply colored pink plastic toy necklace. My stepmother was watching me. I struggled not to show my feelings, but I was still young and tender and relentless tears burst forth. Was that a glimmer of satisfaction I glimpsed in her eyes?

"But Jeanne," she remonstrated for all the family to hear, "we thought you'd love that gift, and we knew it would look stunning on you. I'm sorry, Jeanne, but I just forgot that you wanted the other necklace." How could she forget? I didn't talk about it much, but I was underfoot every day, looking for more work to do. Forget? Not likely.

I asked Joy if she had asked for the pearl set, and she said no, it "didn't matter to her." So then and there I offered to trade my pink plastic necklace for her blue pearl one. She refused, even though I additionally promised her all I had to give in the way of material goods or doing chores for her. There was still a flat "No way!"

"Why would I trade this for that cheap old necklace you got?" she queried. Even she recognized the necklace's tawdry look and rejected acquisition of it.

I never asked for another gift from them, and I never once wore the pink plastic necklace. The entire body of my hope had been ravished by the enemy and left broken, lying in the dust of destroyed desire.

The whole incident was my own fault, I knew, for letting her see the depth of my wanting. No one was ever again going to see what sat so deeply into my heart. It was a vow I kept until I was seventeen.

To this day the blue necklace, my "hangnail in heaven," remains a hangnail in my heart, where every once in a while it snags itself on memory and shoots throbs of pain back to me. I have outgrown blue pearl necklaces … or have I? Do we ever outgrow our blue pearl necklaces? Forgiveness is not forgetfulness.

Chapter Sixteen

FAT AND GRISTLE STEW

When we left Strong's Motel, we moved to Kansas City, where Aunt Alice and Uncle Jack had their beautiful three-story home. Perhaps Daddy thought they would help us, but they knew him too well; we were not invited to move in with them, although we were allowed to stay a week or two until Daddy found a place for us. They made it plain, however, that our time with them was very limited.

We spent about a year in Missouri, all through my ninth year. That was the first year we lived in such an unimaginable situation. The rent in our new home must have been pretty cheap. Where we located was unbelievable, but it was just the first unbelievable place. There were more to come. What we moved into was a basement—the basement of a burned-out house! The rest of the house was gone. The first floor had been replaced and covered with tar paper to serve as our roof and ceiling.

There was only one window, a typical basement window, small, high, and far away. Thus the basement seemed dark and dingy. Even on bright days it felt sinister and dark in there. It was hard to imagine paying any rent to live in this … this *place*. Even then, I couldn't give it the honor of calling it a house or apartment.

One day, thinking of what Grandma would do to pretty up a place, I suggested to my stepmother that if she "got some material to make curtains" for our lone window, it would "make the room prettier." With a snarl her hand flew up to slap me repeatedly across the face. I hadn't meant to insult her; I was just trying to be helpful. That was when I first learned not to make suggestions. They were unwanted, unwelcome, and unacceptable. I was learning that to be silent was to (hopefully) be unnoticed.

To divide our "place" into rooms, Daddy strung up clothesline lengthwise and widthwise across the basement and draped sheets over them, turning the basement into four small rooms. The charred smell of the house seemed to be in every corner of the basement, and I used to lie there in bed with the other kids and wonder if people had burned up in that fire and how we could get out if another fire started. What did it feel like to get burned up by fire? Did you know it for a long time? Could you breathe with all the smoke and smelly things burning? Sometimes it kept me awake. Sometimes I dreamed of burning up, like I used to dream about being buried alive after the baby-sitter took us to the funeral home. A year with Grandma had dimmed those dreams until they disappeared, but there was no Grandma here to wipe out ugly memories or heal frightened suppositions.

Where we lived was an indication of our financial condition. Since we had so little to spend on anything, our food was of the cheapest kind. About every week I'd come home at least once to find that my stepmother had made beef stew.

Perhaps it was "oversupply to our demand," but for some reason I came to hate cooked carrots and canned English peas. As if they weren't bad enough, it seemed as though the stew meat always was mostly fat and gristle. The only thing palatable to me was the potatoes in the stew. I have always loved potatoes; don't ask me why. For some reason they epitomize luxury to me. Perhaps it is the smooth creaminess of mashed potatoes, or maybe I just identified with their being whipped and had great empathy for them. Whatever the reason, I have always loved potatoes: baked potatoes, fried potatoes, boiled potatoes, potatoes in stew, potato salad, mashed potatoes, just potatoes!

One night I trudged home through the snow and cold after school to find that supper was once more the despised stew. I swallowed my disappointment and reminded myself that it wasn't all gristle; there were potatoes in it too. Stepmother always dished the servings out. At first I thought it was accidental, but eventually even I recognized that every stew night she would give me as much of the fat and gristle as she could. She seemed to think it was funny. I know now that sounds paranoid, but it truly wasn't; I had far more than my share of unpalatable, unchewable meat. It was another of her ways of tormenting me. For some reason, my torment seemed to be her happiness.

I tried to eat the stew that night, and I did swallow most of it. I also ate all the potatoes. My stomach rebelled about then and began rolling and heaving. I knew that I couldn't stomach any more stew. That was when Daddy began to yell at me: "Eat the rest!" he stormed. "Eat it, I say! Eat it now, Jeanne. Eat it!" I tried desperately, but every bite I took stuck in my throat and I began to gag. My stomach was braided with knots of pain and fear until I couldn't even swallow. My throat seemed clotted and closed. Then my stomach began to lurch from terror, and helplessly, I vomited into the stew. As I threw up, Daddy shoved my head in the bowl of stew, grabbed his razor strap, and began hitting me harder and harder, yelling like a wild man. The kids began crying and screaming, and even Gil, who was usually my tormentor, began to hold his nose and spoon the stew down his throat. "Eat it like this," he cried, trying to help me, but I couldn't move. By then Daddy had snatched me from the table and began beating me even more fiercely, yelling like a mad man, until I soiled myself, and once again, urine ran down my leg. Little Dolly and Baby John were screaming at the spectacle. Then Daddy forced my jaws open, scooped up the mixture of vomit and stew, and shoveled it down my throat. He forced me to swallow and then wrapped his fingers around my throat to keep me from vomiting it back up. I thought he was trying to choke me.

Finally my stepmother intervened at the sight of his fingers around my throat and told him to stop. Furiously, he banished me from his sight. "Get out of here, you brat, and don't let me see you again tonight. Look at the trouble you've caused!" I stumbled into our corner of the sheet-made room, crawled out of my wet clothes into my old ragged flannel gown, and got under the covers. To him, it was just another insignificant event, quickly forgotten. My life will end before I am able to forget it.

Daddy used to tell about being stationed in France during the war. The French people used to overfeed the geese until they got sick, to make their livers fat. They then put bands around their neck so they couldn't regurgitate. Chinese people do the same thing in reverse. They tie a ring around captive cormorant necks and put them in the water to catch fish. Because they can't swallow the fish, people get it and use it for their own food. The principle is the same: with the throat shut off, what can't be swallowed cannot be eaten or, if already eaten, can't be regurgitated. As to the story of the geese, Daddy's comment was amazement at the lengths the French went to, "all to make paté!" I always wondered if that was where he got the idea to hold my throat closed so I couldn't throw up.

My mind has been vomiting ever since at the memory of that fat and gristle stew, cooked in a barren, burnt-out building with pervasive, charred smells mingling with a little girl's sobs. The smells and sounds roll down through the years like a huge snowball so iced over with terror it is incapable of melting.

My stepmother never made stew again. That episode had been too violent, even for her. It was a kindness from her that I never forgot. Many of her cruelties were undoubtedly deliberate, but once in a while kindness or compassion peeped through. Perhaps she was coping as best she could with such a large family. Perhaps she put Daddy first and her sons and "their" children second and after that, nothing much mattered. Perhaps she was trying to adjust to Daddy's erratic way of life. For whatever reasons, we were forgotten children most of the time. But once in a while when cruelty boiled over in the pot of violence, she would intervene compassionately. This indicates to me that she knew what she was doing when she was so cruel. There was nothing unconscious in what she did. On the other hand, I did not know what it felt like to be married to someone like Daddy. If she had even a scrap of decency in her, it must have abraded her sensitive spots at times, like sandpaper across the skin of an inner place on one's body. But then again, perhaps she enjoyed the cruelties as much as he did. Most often it appeared they were well suited both temperamentally and philosophically. At least they stayed married for years and years.

Memories like that are indelible, and there is no eraser made to expunge them. But there are things that help. My inner determination to "never, never ever treat any of my children like that" was one maxim that kept me from derailing on the track of child torture. Another determination was to "always make my children feel loved and wanted." That was a resolution that grew like steel within the core of my self. Those goals perhaps were the things that kept me from becoming an abuser myself, as so many abused children are. I never wanted anyone to feel as I was being made to feel. Sometimes our very prison bars are the things that, in the end, set us free.

Chapter Seventeen

BLUE ICE CASTLES

My parents divorced when we were still small. I was four, Joy was three, and Ray was one. After we were shuttled back and forth from baby-sitter to baby-sitter while in Mother's care, and then lived with Grandma and Grandpa Love for a year, our father was forced to take us, so off we went to Arizona where we ended up as unwanted burdens to him. Life with father was a new kind of existence of horror, but one thing stayed the same: we moved from place to place, never staying long in any one spot. By the time I was nearly eight we had been moved from Tallahassee to Stewart, Florida, to two places in Arizona to Missouri, where we lived in poverty.

One thing happened in Missouri to make the drabness of my existence turn to light for a little while. When I was eight and in the third grade my teacher announced that we were going to make a beautiful ice castle. Empty boxes of all sizes and shapes were brought in by the class and covered with flour and water paste. The addition of blue food coloring and salt for glitter gave it color and sparkle.

This was this most exciting thing a skinny little third grader had ever seen. I could hardly wait to get to school! My enthusiasm was contagious. "Let's color this cardboard like stones and put them on top of the moat," I would energetically suggest. (I had invented a moat and bridge for the castle.) "Let's make a fire-eating dragon!" I'd shout. What my stepmother disparagingly called my "wild hair ideas" was really my creativity pumping madly, attempting to burst forth. My enthusiasm was caught by the class, and our beautiful castle grew more regal every day. The class's creation was the most beautiful thing I had ever seen. It was also the first time I remembered having a sense of self-worth. I was helping to make something that people admired and others wanted to help with!

Whenever anyone finished her assignments she could work on the castle. I loved it, not only because of the beauty of the castle, but because I quickly learned the paste could be eaten and that it made my hungry stomach quit hurting. One night sitting around the dinner table Daddy noticed my bright blue tongue and lips. He asked what we were doing in school, and I explained with all the excitement and enthusiasm that bubbled inside me at the very thought of the ice castle. It had become a magic castle to me. Hungry, ill-dressed, poorly housed, my world nevertheless had a magic aspect in it because of my ice castle.

"Let me see your tongue again," Daddy said. In all innocence, I showed him. He gave a muted exclamation. "You have a terrible disease," he declared.

"What is it?" I stammered.

"It's called blue tongue disease."

"W-Will you take me to the doctor, Daddy?"

"Well … it wouldn't do any good. It's a disease that's deadly. You'll probably die tonight. Besides, if I take you to the doctor, it will cost money. You don't want me to waste the money on you that I might need for the other kids when you'll soon be dead, do you?" He said that would be selfish. I was ashamed.

Alone and desolate, I put on my old flannel nightgown and went to bed, waiting to die. I lay on the bed all evening, picking at the holes in my nightgown, waiting and wondering what it felt like to die. Would I go to heaven? Would anyone miss me? Would anyone be sad if I died? Suddenly, I became aware of other voices intruding upon my thoughts. My stepmother and father were laughing, talking about what they would do when I died. Daddy said any old box would do and it needn't be very big either. I heard my stepbrother Gil suggest that they just throw me in the river. Undoubtedly they knew I was listening.

"Oh no," said Daddy. "That would be mean! We will bury her in the backyard under the snow."

That answered two questions: no one would be sad to see me die and no one would miss me.

Sometime in the night I fell into a fitful restless sleep. In the morning I woke up to discover that I was still alive! Fearful of when death would come, I dragged out to the kitchen and said something to my stepmother, only to see a smirk on her face. She knew that I would soon be dead, I supposed. I didn't bother to eat that morning. Why eat my meager portion if I was going to die?

The walk to school always seemed uphill. I hated it. Rubber boots are the coldest footwear in the world, and my thin clothes let the wind and cold through as if they didn't exist. At least I wouldn't have to worry about being cold again, I thought as I trudged along, and I wouldn't have to wear those awful rubber galoshes! I had outgrown my pair of shoes, and we couldn't afford another pair.

Because of a lack of shoes I would wear those galoshes all day every day in Arizona and Missouri and until we moved to Florida, where I could go barefoot. But I didn't know that then. All I knew was I wouldn't have to be cold much longer.

Another bright spot in the day was when the teacher gave us the math assignment. Oh, how I hated and feared arithmetic! But this time I didn't have to care!

"I don't have to do the assignment," I confided to the teacher, "because I probably won't live to finish it."

"Whatever do you mean, child?"

"I have a terrible disease called blue tongue disease. My Daddy says it will kill me today. Really, I should have died last night, he said."

"Oh, my dear, I'm sure they were only joking. Why did they tell you had—what did you call it?—blue tongue disease?"

"They saw my blue tongue."

"How did your tongue get blue?"

"It was from eating the paste."

"Oh!" she said knowingly. "Perhaps it is a good idea not to eat so much of the paste, but I promise you it will not kill you." I could tell that she was speaking the truth. I wasn't going to die! I felt relief beyond belief. I also felt a bit stupid as I sat trying to puzzle out why I had been told by my own father and family that I was going to die. It was then that my heart got lost in horror. Now I understood. The family knew what they had done; they did it on purpose because they wanted me to think I was dying! I was humiliated and hurt. How they must be laughing at me!

There was no talking those days about "depression," and all I knew was that life became a period of sadness for me. Living was drab and filled with hurt and fear. Betrayal hurts as much at seven years of age as at seventy. My entire life was affected. I never touched the wonderful ice castle again. Without my wild ideas to build a drawbridge with chains and the moat and fire-breathing dragons, my classmates quit adding to it also.

One day the teacher asked, "Is anyone going to work on the castle anymore?" She looked straight at me. As my eyes met hers, I shook my head no. The ice castle now represented pain and rejection. Death and humiliation had become associated with it. Everyone else had quite building on it when I did, so eventually it was dismantled and taken away.

The days all became gray days. There was nothing to look forward to, and looking backward I had only eight years of scarred memories that I avoided—all my life except our year on the farm. The rest was remembered pain sometimes so great that I could taste it, smell it, feel it. "You have to be taught to be afraid," the song from South Pacific goes. I can remember being taught to fear.

Sometimes memory can be a curse.

It's a simple story of a family teasing a little girl. But is it really? Is it "teasing" when the subject is a serious and personal one like death? Is it teasing to let it go on for hours or even overnight? Is it teasing when the scars of that event linger on in the mind of an adult, tied to the twin hitching posts of pain and memory? Or is it abuse? If the teasing would cause pain for someone, blemish his self-esteem or image, undermine her confidence, it is not teasing; it is abuse. I can hear some people now, saying, "Every kid has to learn to be teased. He's got to be tough about it and learn to tease back." Or, "It's just the way fellas show affection. You don't understand; it's a 'man' thing." Oh, really? And how do we know what perception that child will carry away? His experiences are not ours. Can we crawl into the attic of his head to find what will be stored there? How can we possibly know how anyone else will perceive and react? Isn't it better to be on the safe side and avoid the possibility of wounding, of causing lasting scars? Is it really so hard to avoid the cruel, demeaning, downputting, undercutting remark? This is where our hidden abuse comes from. That is where the unsuspecting abuser must finally meet and confront himself. It is a very hard moment to honestly confront. But it may save someone's future from the ashpits of despair or the belief that she is a "born loser" if we are brave enough to confront ourselves. Few of us want to make ashes of someone's innocence or trust; yet, almost all of us do it unconsciously, at times. The question is, how many dare admit it ... or attempt to change it?

Chapter Eighteen

OLD MISSY

When I was eight going on nine, Daddy moved us all from Missouri to Sopchoppy, Florida, his home town. He found work in the lumber mill there. We had no money and nowhere to live, but Daddy's brother, Uncle Delbert, owned a tobacco barn where he let us stay. This, our second unbelievable house in a row, was to become home for almost a year. Every day our little cousins—one especially—would greet us with the refrain "Dis ah bacca bahn!" We were considered interlopers; it was *their* barn, and we were there only by their family's generosity.

The tobacco barn was a newly built building, but it was still a barn. There were no rooms save one partitioned area where the tobacco was hung to dry. That's where Joy, Ray, and I were to sleep. There was no glass or screens in the windows, but at least there wasn't a scorched, burned-out smell to the building, as there had been in our Missouri basement place. On the hot steamy days of a Florida summer, mosquitoes and flies must have thought we were a major recreation area. For the humans within, it was tortuous living, but it had a great redeeming aspect to me. At night as I lay on my pallet under the open window hoping to catch an occasional brush of breeze, I could see the stars and sometimes the moon. I'd fall asleep counting stars. The night sky became an enchanted land where I could slip from the horrible *now* into a wonderful *someday*. It became a reason for enduring.

Then one day, Daddy came home with rolls of tarpaulin in his arms. We asked what it was for. His only reply was "Wait and see!" The next day we hurried home to hear hammer sounds coming from the barn. Daddy was nailing tarp over the door and every window. When you needed privacy you rolled the tarp down. Daytimes, the tarp was rolled up. During the day, living continued to be an agony of biting, and at night the loose wavy tarp seemed only to be a challenge to the mosquitoes, which apparently considered the barn a restaurant and me a menu item labeled "Free Food." Daddy had one more improvement to make: he moved a cook stove in. Once again we could have warm food to eat. After a steady diet of cold food day after day, that cook stove was a miracle to our young eyes.

As for furniture, there were beds for Stepmother and Daddy, Lee, Gil, Dolly, and even John, the new baby. There were none for us, however. I guess it was because they were people and people deserve beds. At no time during my years with Jean and Daddy were we ever made to feel like people. We were not considered "human beings;" We became known as "the Burdens." Somehow I understood that "Burdens" were not really people. The proof to me was that I never met any real people by that name.

There were some chairs and a table in their room too, but we—Joy, Ray, and I—slept, sat, and ate on the floor. We were the family "its," the Burdens who deserved nothing. There was no electricity, so we had no fans for summer and, except for that little wood cook stove, no heat for winter. My wonderful world of starlight and *someday* was gone; taken from me by a thick, moldy-smelling tarp. But with our move to the "bacca" barn, a relationship I had already established became a central part of my world that compensated for everything else. It was alive, it was *now,* and it loved me devotedly. It was Old Missy.

Old Missy, a gold-colored cocker spaniel, had been Lee and Gil's dog for years in Arizona. She still slept with them at night and followed all of us at play by day, but after the incident with the sugar bowl, it seemed that Old Missy was my special protector. She stuck by my side when we were playing, and if anyone was too rough with me, she would jump at them and tug at their clothes. My playmates made sure she was not around the times when I was sexually molested by them or when I was raped.

At age seven, I was still malnourished and much too thin. Old Missy seemed to sense my fragility, inside and out. She was always with me, and I used her as a best friend, talking to her and petting and playing with her endlessly. It made Lee and Gil angry, but they couldn't do anything about it.

Summer swung by in long lazy loops of heat, humidity, mosquitoes, and floor-living, punctuated by laughter and play, with Old Missy in the midst of it all. Soon enough school time swooped upon us like migrating bursts of birds riding feather-light autumn winds. Once again we would enter a strange school where we would be looked upon as "new people" and I would be seen as a person with strange ears, funny freckles, and a skinny body. But this school had some compensations; it seemed to almost welcome us! This was the little wooden schoolhouse where Daddy and our aunts and uncles had gone. My grandma Jerry planted the roses there from a cutting her ma had. All those years later it was still blooming! I felt very protective toward that rose bush. Here at last, in this old country school, I recognized my roots and felt that I could comfortably slip into one of the spaces left by ghosts of students past.

A fine old wooden building, it was redolent of the passage of time, trials, and trysts. An auditorium and lunchroom made it larger than most country schools, but all I remember is a couple of classrooms. Moss Hill Country Church near Vernon, Florida, reminds me of it today. Some of the ceilings and walls hold the resined foot and palm prints of people—blacks, probably—who originally built the edifices. Or farmers with hands spiked by calluses, shopkeepers more used to silk than saws? Husky teens growing into manhood? I like to imagine what they looked like; how many children they had; whether they were slave or free. Now only fingerprints and footprints are left, burned into boards by resin mixed with sweat and labor. I used to think like that about the old schoolhouse, too, wondering who built it. I was an ever-curious kid.

Marching around the schoolhouse was an old split-rail fence the principal's daddy had built for the school fifty years before. My grandma Jerry's roses grew nearby. It was the year of my ninth birthday. One of the best teachers I ever had was there. She was kind and gentle and remains imprinted on my memory forever, as kindness and gentleness often are. It was our loss when she left to become a missionary. I couldn't see why she had to leave to do missionary work; we could have generated enough challenges for her.

One day we were all shoved outside for a fire drill. Minutes later the smell of smoke told us this wasn't a fire drill; this was for real! The split-rail fence was on fire! Old wood burning makes its own sharp smell, which lingers on in my memory to this day. It was a day of confusion, flames, fear, and ultimately, a great sadness as we watched some of the town's history burning. Firemen and volunteers from town came racing to control the fire. Some were pulling up the old split-rail fence and piling the pieces safely aside to be rebuilt. As the headmistress-principal cried and sobbed into her hanky, she said that her daddy had helped build that school, and she'd taught there many years. She lost more than history on that sad day; she lost a remembered part of her life. But the fire didn't spread, so the schoolhouse was saved and to this day holds the glue of history in its very beams.

After the fire was out we kids were all sent home so they could survey the damage without us underfoot. You know kids; any excuse for a holiday. This one, however, was met with subdued voices and quiet steps. No one raced home that day. Some kids got to ride the bus, but we lived within a mile, so we walked.

Usually as we trudged along on the way to school, I'd fill my little metal lard-can "lunch-bucket" with wild berries to eat at noon. Old Missy would follow us to school wagging her tail, and at the end of the road we'd tell her, "Go home, Missy!" (And she did). She understood so much! At the end of the day when school was out, we'd find Old Missy waiting beside the road, tail wagging and backside wiggling impatiently, a golden spot in the dust and dirt of the road. Just once she came onto the school grounds and the headmistress scolded us. We showed Missy where not to pass, explaining why all the while, and it was as if she knew. She waited off the roadside after that. Eventually we were able to go to school again with the rebuilt fence in view, rising like a phoenix from its former perished ashes.

One day after school we scampered home to play out under the far side of the house by the swamp. Close by, Old Missy frolicked in the sunshine. Uncle Delbert had cleared a small area in front and along part of the sides of the tobacco barn, but the back sides and rear of the barn stood on stilts about six feet tall above the murky waters. The back was heavily wooded with cedar and cypress. Under them lay the ominous black swamp, glassy, heavy, and fetid.

This day we kids were playing around the wooded area when suddenly Old Missy began to bark. It was a different bark, shrill and urgent. We looked over and there, sidling up to Lee, we saw a cottonmouth water moccasin. We stood paralyzed as it coiled and struck at Lee. Instantly springing in front of him and knocking him to the ground, Old Missy gave a big yelp as the snake struck her in the throat across the jugular. Old Missy had saved Lee's life. Lee was the oldest and biggest boy, and he picked Missy up and carried her into the clearing.

We all sat beside her, crying and sobbing. Aunt Ruby and Uncle Delbert heard our commotion and came running. Uncle Delbert told Daddy that he should use his shotgun to put her out of her misery. Daddy gave the excuse that "my wife wouldn't let me do it." There was no money to take her to the veterinarian. No one knew what to do. We just stood there. Old Missy tried a few times to stand up and fell each time. Her life was fading. Because of being bitten in the jugular the venom hit her bloodstream immediately, and white foam came from her mouth. We kept trying to wipe it away. Finally her eyes began to change and her breathing grew labored. Daddy said she wasn't suffering anymore; she was going into a coma. Where at first she'd recognized us now she didn't. We kids kept frantically trying to give her a drink of water to clear her throat. Finally Lee lay down on the ground beside her with his arm around her, just like they slept, so she'd die happy.

Little Dolly was screaming, and my stepmother, who arrived last, was holding her. Daddy held Little John, our newest baby brother. The children were grouped around Ole Missy's inert body on the ground, crying and sobbing and stroking her fur. We were telling her, "It'll be all right, Missy," when suddenly with a violent shudder and a strange whoosh of air Old Missy was gone. In her dying, Old Missy had done something that had never happened before; she drew us together as a family unit. Finally we were one, united in a common concern. I do not remember ever seeing this again.

Once again, at Old Missy's death, my small world had been crushed. It had been a different world when there was something there that loved me and would protect me. If adults later were to say I anthropomorphized her, well so what? She was real and precious to me and was more loving than any human except my grandparents had ever been. Now she too was gone, and only fragile, tenuous memories were left to hold on to. My days were filled with a quiet sadness and a deep sense of being alone again. There were no wet licks on my face; no one glad to see me. Life was so lonesome with no one to love. Old Missy, my protector, my very best friend, was gone. Then I realized that so was a lot else in my life. Innocence, trust, hope, and a sense of justice were all violated the day Old Missy died. I thought goodness would eventually always be rewarded, that justice would protect the good, that you could "trust in God" like our money said, that hopes were good dreams to have. Old Missy's death seemed to disprove all that.

It was some time after Old Missy's death that Lee and Gil's father and stepmother came from Arizona to visit the boys. Looking forward to their visit helped ease the lonely ache. We counted the days until their arrival. Finally they were here! This was not to be the joyous experience we anticipated, however. When they saw where Lee and Gil were living they were horrified. They toured the barn and said, "This is no way for kids to live." I couldn't understand what the fuss was about; Lee and Gil had beds and all that other furniture to use. They could sit in a chair, eat from a table, and lie in a bed, because they were *people*. They were the lucky ones, we thought, but Strong didn't see it that way. As soon as they got the boys packed up they immediately left for Phoenix, Lee and Gil waving stunned good-byes from the backseat.

A few hours after the boys left I was in the front yard with a washboard and metal washtub, rubbing soap on clothes, one of my chores. My stepmother came over, crying, because the boys had gone. She was always telling us we were just extra mouths to feed; extra washing, ironing, and work to do. In other words, we were Burdens. As she approached me I asked in all innocence, "Why are you crying? I thought you'd be happy because it's two less mouths to feed and clean up after." I hadn't realized that the burden part applied only to Joy, Ray, and me; not to Lee and Gil. She made sure I understood it.

We were to spend nearly a year in the tobacco barn without furniture of any kind except the cookstove, beds, table, and chairs. Being "Burdens," we weren't allowed to use them, however. Our bed clothes were still spread on the floor at night, even after Gil and Lee left. Beds were now available for us, but we couldn't sleep in them. Neither were we allowed to sit on the chairs they had used or eat at the table with the others. It wasn't about availability; it was about defining what (not who) we were. Beds, tables, and chairs were for them but not for us—for people, not for Burdens, not for nonhumans.

Obediently, the three of us sat, ate, and drank down on the floor. We were fed, bedded, and apparently wedded to the floors of our home. Mosquitoes continued to drone, the swamp continued to smell heavy and fetid, and the sight of the gummy swamp waters brought only memories of cottonmouthed poison. Playing outside was no longer fun, but being indoors meant being captive to biting insects. There was no good choice. Once more, there was nowhere to turn. Nowhere. A hard lesson to learn, at age nine.

Chapter Nineteen

DENIED AND REJECTED

One day while we were still living in the old tobacco barn, Daddy announced that he had to go to Tallahassee to pick up a part for the old pickup.

My heart immediately felt like the pin prickles you get after your foot, gone to sleep, begins to wake up. I was waking up inside! I begged to go see our real mother, who lived in Tallahassee and whom we had not seen since her unfortunate fainting episode after she'd flown to Arizona to see us. By then about two or two and a half years had passed with no cards, no letters, no visits.

Joy and Ray, one and two years my junior, began to clamor to go also. Daddy barked, "Okay, okay! Snap to it; get ready!" No electricity meant no iron, so our clothes were naturally wrinkled, but we dressed ourselves as best we could and clambered into the old truck, chattering with excitement. Off we drove to Tallahassee, three little heads barely able to peek over the dashboard of the old pickup. We were going to see Mother!

Daddy, dressed in his old overalls, saw us to the front door of a very large beautiful house. I saw him knock, even though all I could hear was my own skinny knees knocking with fear and excitement. Then he turned and walked away, leaving us standing there.

Little Ray's hair, newly combed and wet, stuck up in a cowlick. He stood sturdily, hands in the pockets of his outgrown overalls. Joy and I, thinking we looked "dressed up" in our unironed clothes, were really probably pretty deplorable looking. Daringly, when no one answered Daddy's knock, I rang the bell. As the door opened I heard Daddy's truck start up and drive away. A black lady towered over us at the door. She wore a white cap, a white apron, and a black dress.

"What yo want?" she asked suspiciously.

"We're here to see our Mother, Edna," I said in my best eight-year-old voice.

"Miss Edna ain't said nothing about no chilun. Mr. Harry ain't said nothing either."

Nevertheless she opened the door a bit wider and in we stepped, quick as the blink of a lizard's eye. The maid was helpless, not knowing how to handle this unexpected situation. We knew Miss Edna's name, which gave us some credence. What to do? Nothing had prepared her for the appearance of three waifs from wherever, wrapped in expectation and clothed in wrinkles with bits of cloth in between, just walking into her living room.

Putting my best foot forward in my cracked patent leather shoes, I looked around. After the chill wind and bright sunlight outdoors, the inside looked like the castle in a little girl's dreams. Lambent light from a crystal chandelier graced across an elegant marble coffee table. Pale blue walls and deeper blue carpet created a peaceful interplay of monochromaticism. Sheer curtains that let sunlight through in lacelets of light were framed by draperies of white silk on the sides and valance. The aura of effulgent whiteness was punctuated by beautiful French furniture and mirrors.

Speechless, I stood in awe. Never had I seen such beauty, such elegance, and this was my mother's house! It was the most exquisite thing my dazzled eyes had ever seen. My eyes continued to move until they came to rest on a tray. It held Coca Colas in green glass bottles. I remembered drinking "Coke" like that once, long ago. Sitting beside the tray of Cokes were trays of tiny sandwiches, petit fours, and cakes. It was as if they expected us! How had they known? We had come to a party just for us! It was a little girl's dream of Mother. All my deepest dreams had come true! My elegant mother lived in a refined home, and she was welcoming us with a joie de vivre party! A party just for us, her very own children! My heart soared so high into atmospheric happiness that it felt as if it would explode.

I asked again for our mother and then requested the Coke and food. Could we please have some? The maid answered that they were having a dedication party and the food was for the guests. My joy stuttered like a faulty plane. Weren't we the guests? It was then that the joy began to dissolve like butter left out in a hot sun. Were we interlopers instead of guests?

"I s'pose you kin have one Coke," she said dubiously as she turned and began filling three paper cups instead of using the elegant crystal goblets on the trays.

"What do I do with these chil'run?" she muttered to herself. Before we could drink our Coke a tall man came in the door carrying a blanket-wrapped bundle.

Handing the bundle gingerly to the maid he saw us and said, "What are these ... children ... doing here? We have guests coming!"

As the oldest of the three I stepped forward and said, "We've come to see our mother, Edna. Daddy had to go get a part for the pickup, and we came to see our mother." The man blanched and then turned red. The red crept up his neck all the way into his hair.

Turning to the maid he commanded her to "get these ragamuffin children into the kitchen and keep them out of sight until I get Edna out of the car."

He went to the car. Just then the forgotten bundle in the maid's arms let out a mewling peep. I scrambled to see. Before the maid could stop me I had pushed back the blanket to see a wrinkled fair-haired new baby. Eagerly I reached out to touch the tiny baby, only to be pushed away and told not to touch. It was Edna and Harry's new baby, and I "might have germs." Just then Harry walked in, carrying my mother in his arms as you carry a new bride. We weren't in the kitchen as we were supposed to be, so Mother saw us immediately! She was as beautiful as ever to me. Her jet black hair, shocking blue eyes, and the pale blue quilted robe and the fuzzy mule slippers with high heels she wore made the whole scene frozen in time by my memory. What happened next helped freeze events forever in my mind and heart.

Mother gasped and turned pale as Harry demanded to know who we were. "Edna, who are these children? Whose are they? They say they came to see their mother! 'Their mother Edna!'"

Mother began sobbing and cried, "I was afraid you wouldn't want to marry me if you knew I had children." Abruptly he set her down. At that very moment Daddy pulled up in the old pickup, just as a long gray Cadillac arrived! The baby began crying in the maid's arms, and my mother was sobbing and "ruining her makeup." Daddy parked the old truck at the curb and honked, just as the first guests were coming up the walk. Suddenly Harry's hands were a vise on Joy and my skinny little forearms as we were abruptly marched to the porch.

"You are upsetting your mother," he gritted, teeth clenched.

"I want to have a word with your father before you all leave," he growled.

"Edna, straighten yourself up. We've company coming up the walk. We'll discuss this later."

Abruptly Harry walked to the truck with one of us under each big hand, Ray tagging along behind. Daddy saw us coming and got out to lean insolently against the truck as Joy, Ray, and I climbed inside. Harry upbraided Daddy for bringing us without letting them know anything in advance.

"We are having a reception and dedication of our new baby!" he gritted, strain in every tone. "These ragamuffins have no place here!"

I was overcome with emotion at getting to see my mother after nearly three years only to receive no hugs, no kisses, no words of welcome, and not even a visit. But ... Mother was not glad to see us. She didn't even want us to be her children!

We never got to drink our Coke or eat one of the pretty little cakes. The party obviously was not for us, and we were not wanted here. I was a kaleidoscope of emotions, riding a roller coaster of insight. My elation knew no bounds at seeing Mother. She was my ideal, my role model, the bright star of all my horizons, my queen. Nearly everything I had done for years had been measured against whether she would approve of it or not. She was my idol. I had been idolizing a woman who wanted nothing to do with me! Who had denied my very existence! There will never be enough time, enough words, to describe those moments. They sit heavy as immoveable iron in a wild sea. They are the soggy dirty laundry of leftover dreams that I once wore.

I was found lacking and had been rejected. From that moment on I made a conscious effort to discard my fantasies and dreams of my mother. It would prove to be a lifelong challenge of learning to accept the pain of rejection, the concept of unworthiness, the hell of inadequacy. Dreams don't die easily; they linger, perhaps slumbering for years before erupting in mountainous volcanic pain once again. I would spend most of a lifetime trying to accept my mother's rejection, wondering where I was deficient, where I had failed. There is no pain greater than the pain of rejected love, no fracture greater then a broken dream, no pit deeper than a child's disillusionment.

Only later did it dawn on me that my father had laughed all the way home. He was jovial, happy, excited. He'd glance at his little "ragamuffin" kids and just laugh and laugh. I heard him telling Stepmother about it when we got home. He and she had a great time laughing about it.

That was when I began to realize that our pain was their joy.

Chapter Twenty

GENES AND GENEALOGY

When we moved back to Tempe, Arizona, from Florida, Daddy began work at the navy base as an electrician. He found an old house in Tempe and rented it. Granddaddy Bush, my stepmother's dad, moved back from Mr. and Mrs. Hall's where he boarded during the time we'd been in Missouri and then in Sopchoppy, Florida, for a year. When Granddaddy came back to live with us he brought cousin Warren, Uncle Dick's firstborn son.

Uncle Dick was an enigma of a man. Born of Granddaddy and Grandma Bush, he was always sickly. Eventually he married a Mexican woman he met. She bore him one child, Warren, before Uncle Dick died. In fact, even before he died but after they separated, she continued to bear Uncle Dick many children! Being a barfly and a mother didn't mix, however, and it became apparent that she didn't want the responsibility of a young child. Warren was another maternally unwanted child. When I first knew him, he was a big heavyset boy with a terrible complex about having his mother's dark Mexican complexion. He was about thirteen years old. Racial prejudice had already been placed in his perceptions through the indifference of his mother. Life begins forming us at the moment of birth.

The head count at the old house had increased again with Granddaddy's reentry. There were now Daddy and Stepmother, Lee and Gil (hers), Jeanne, Joy, Ray (his), Dolly and John (theirs), plus Granddaddy and Warren—eleven people underfoot every day! Sometimes the count reduced itself by two because Gil and Lee spent about half their time with us and half with their Dad, Strong.

That was a lot of people to put their feet under the table. For years Daddy had gone to night school besides working full-time. He was truly a brilliant man who could do anything he set his mind to. He built rooms, did concrete work, electrical work, plumbing; whatever the situation called for he could figure it out.

When Dolly wanted to play the glockenspiel and began taking lessons, he looked at her books every night after school and had her explain what the teacher taught that day. We thought he was just checking her, making sure she learned her lessons, until the day he sat down, picked up the metal-barred instrument, and began playing a tune on it with the two hammers. He learned to play it well.

Like a fast-flowing energetic young river, he never quit moving along, and soon he left the banks of the beautifully belled glockenspiel for a pianoed channel of the river where soft chords and thundering basses lured him on. He began bringing books home at night and taught himself to play piano and organ. He played those well too! He could do whatever he set his mind to.

When he went into business for himself he became known on Dun and Bradstreet as the owner of the electric company that did the most business during that particular year. He made thousands, but we still lived in poverty because he gave so many customers credit that was never paid. We were poor in person and rich on paper.

When Daddy was in the tenth grade he'd had to go to work to help support the family. His daddy, Grandfather Jerry, was a farmer, with about six hundred acres in the beginning. Daddy was one of twelve children. Back then, the more children a farmer had the more prosperous he could become, because he had more workers. Granddaddy Jerry had been orphaned at the age of five. He'd been farmed out by his older brothers to help earn money to live. He followed a mule and plow all day. When he grew up he married a woman named Cleopatra. Granddaddy Jerry was a small man, as was his bride, Cleopatra. Granddaddy had grown up hard, but his word was his bond; he'd become a well-respected man.

Granddad and Cleopatra had three children. Shortly after the third one, Uncle Bill, was born Granddad came in from the fields tired and dusty to see Grandma lying in bed. Back then they felt that a woman's feet shouldn't hit the floor till ten days after childbirth, but Granddad didn't hold with such nonsense. Aunt Marge and Aunt Cleo were only about three and two and had to be taken care of. Uncle Bill was three days old. There was food to be cooked and meals to serve. Work was waiting! Granddad chewed her out for "lying in here in bed resting while I'm in the fields working like a dog."

We'll never know if she was motivated by anger, humiliation, or guilt, but for whatever reasons, Cleopatra got up immediately and went to work in the field with him. She quietly hemorrhaged to death in the row beside him, trying to keep up with the pace he set. She never complained or said a word. She had to know what was happening! Was this her way of shedding more responsibility than she could bear? Did she feel trapped, penned in by circumstances that would forever chew at her? Animals will chew off a paw to escape a trap; her "paw" was her life's blood, and apparently she was willing to lose it to escape the trap she found herself in.

How desperate she must have been to willingly leave a three-day old infant and two little girls behind! What did she think; how did she feel as she bled to death in the fields that day? We will never know. Cleopatra's desperation and despair are an ink-and-paper item now rather than flesh and blood.

Her story is simply a thinning part of family history. None of us will ever know how it must have been to feel her life's blood pumping out of herself or to have a toil-hardened husband work beside her without ever noticing that she was dying, leaving puddles of blood soaking into the dry soil beneath. Nor will we ever know what Granddad's true feelings were that day, but we do know that he proclaimed he'd never invite a wife of his to the fields again so soon after childbirth.

Grandma Cleopatra had a cousin, a single woman who heard about the death and came to stay and care for the children. In those days necessity, not love, was often the basis of a marriage. It was no surprise then that eventually she and Granddad got married. If love was small to start with it one might surmise that it grew in some ways, since together they had nine more children, some of whom died at birth.

True to his word, Granddad never allowed her back to the fields until her full ten days were up and she came on her own. I still remember the sight of Grandpa, starched white shirt and black slacks, Bible in his hand, ready for church. He was a devout Christian, hard-working, stern, without any surplus of humor, just—as he perceived justice—demanding but fair—as he saw fairness—a product of his time and his genes. Granddad and Grandma Jerry, my father's parents, are buried in a little country graveyard near the great "Bend" of Florida where the Peninsula tears itself away from the Panhandle to stand alone, perpendicular to the east-west lid of the state. Beside their graves lie the graves of my two sons, Trey and Jim. My father's grave is now at their feet.

The fact that learning came easy made it hard for Daddy to understand someone who struggled. That is why he was so intolerant of my fear of math. His attitudes salted and peppered my penchants and perceptions. Once our life orientations are encased in the iron jackets of our parents' attitudes there is little room for reversal unless we are willing to take the chrysalis of change upon ourselves and struggle to break out into the transformation of our own being. It is a difficult task.

We never had nice furniture. Sometimes we had almost none. This old house was no exception. Daddy's ability to do so many things once again came to the rescue. With so many people to feed we needed a place to eat. Daddy built a huge table for us and made benches for each side. A chair stood at each end to give us more room. While it would never be regarded as the work of a master craftsman, it was certainly adequate, and served the purpose.

When Granddaddy Bush came back to live with us (we needed his Social Security money), one of the conditions was that he could bring all his books. He had hundreds and hundreds of hardbound books, a very cosmopolitan assortment on every subject including even some children's books.

A whole new world opened up before me as I read aloud to Dolly and John, or to myself if they abandoned the "reading post." Granddad also brought his "Old Vic" Victrola with its brass arm that held the needle and the winding crank. It was a fascinating thing! The old '78 records were of operas in another language, and there was one ballet and numerous classical records. There was even an old Rudy Valle, which was badly warped. Daddy promised that he could bring the books, but there was no place in the house for them! By this time our versatile Daddy had already built a big covered porch across the back of the old house. His solution to the book problem was simply to add shelving out there. He built wall-to-wall bookcases across two walls out on the roofed porch. This held most of the books, although some were still in boxes. I began reading, voraciously and indiscriminately.

In the afternoons, after school, I'd sneak out to the old Victrola, wind it, and place some of the records on. The old opera, sung in a language I didn't know and couldn't understand, nevertheless stirred my soul and touched some chord inside me that resonated with my very soul. I would then squat on the floor with my ear to the side as I cranked. I didn't want to miss a note.

The music and the singers had such great power to move me that tears would roll down my cheeks or joy well up inside me, depending on the music. When I closed my eyes I could see the singers on the stage. The ballet affected me the same way. There was recognition inside me then; a knowing of something still unknown yet somehow felt, something that would forever be a part of my destiny. Where do artistic genes come from when there were no known artist ancestors? Genes will "out." Perhaps some genes had split or maybe coalesced. Or perhaps God sprinkles gene dust on us while we sleep in the womb. Daddy told me to leave the Victrola alone. He said I was warping the records. Actually it was the outdoor location that most likely was responsible. He built rows and rows of shelves out on the roofed porch, until it looked like the town library. The problem was that even though they were covered above, wind and rain could blow in to touch the books with chill, damp fingers of decay.

Eventually the weather took its toll, even though the Arizona climate helped preserve the books beyond normal expectation. I loved the books. Granddaddy Bush had every kind of subject you could imagine. I read voraciously, transported to other times and places. That's when I really learned what a magic wonderland reading was. A reader can be anything, go anywhere, become anyone he is reading about. He can move through time or space. He can be a physical superman or a spiritual being without visibility or substance. If reading is the universal wonder of our history, then the reader is our time traveler.

Not only did I spend a great deal of time out on the back porch, but I played school under it a lot. John and Dolly both required much entertaining, so I taught them at my "school." I taught Dolly to write her name when she was little and to read. John wasn't in school yet, but I worked with him too. I was eleven years old, and I taught as I thought right. Repetition was the order of the day, so I repeated and repeated. I only had a few children's books, so that's what we used. They never seemed to mind the drilling. I was continually dreaming up new ways of teaching them. Finally, unnoticed by the adults, I had earned some sort of authority, even if it was only with John and Dolly. It was a wondrous change. It also had its practical benefits. Dolly began reading! It was time for writing lessons. Over and over while they took naps I would make dot-to-dots of their names. Dolly picked hers up easily, but John had great difficulty learning to print his name. Soon, though, he was reading, and he hadn't even entered kindergarten yet! Thus, learning slipped in unnoticed as we played our games. Every day I'd play school with them until John would beg to go elsewhere to play and would run off. Stepmother always let him go, if he wanted. I, of course, preferred to keep my captives in school with me.

Some time after they entered "real school" it was discovered that they were both way ahead of the other children. Now in all fairness, I must admit that it probably wasn't mainly due to my teaching. When they were IQ-tested later at school, Dolly was in the 140s and John was in the 170s. John was still having difficulty writing, so he was tested about that. It was then that they discovered that his thinking went so far ahead, so fast, that he couldn't slow his mind down enough to write well. John became an RN and emergency room supervisor at a big hospital. He takes night courses because he wants to become an anesthetist. When John was born I wasn't allowed to hold him like I had Dolly. They didn't want him crying for me, wanting to be held by me, like she had. I loved John, but not like Dolly, because I'd taken care of her so much when she was little.

Dolly went to college first, majoring in computer programming; later she switched to a general business degree. She's a head booker for Ethan Allen Galleries now. She and her husband also run a highly successful hearing aid company. When Dolly got pregnant with her only son, Brian, the obstetrician hospitalized her immediately. She was ready to go into a diabetic coma. We never knew she was diabetic. She had a difficult time and never had another child. Often, genetics play a part in diabetes. Genes and genealogy—how affected we are by them! And yet there is so much we can change, nevertheless.

Our cousin Warren died of pneumonia when he was grown.

My sister Joy became an RN. She had two children: one son, Junior, in law school, and a daughter, Teresa, who after finishing college became a teacher and is currently working on her master's. Joy put up with an abusive husband for many, many years. In fact, he was one of good old Joe's buddies, and Joe introduced them. Joe, my first husband and an unbelievable part of my history, was yet to come. His story will be part of another book.

My brother Ray, only one year old when my real mother and father divorced, is, I think, the hardest hit of all. He married a girl from Puerto Rico. When their marriage broke up he turned to drinking. Ray became an electrician gifted in the sense that Daddy was, able to figure out how things work and invent things to fix it. Roy's wife, Zoila, was mean. She held the children over his head, bribing him with visitation threats when they were growing up, blaming him for all that is not good, berating him, never giving him any positive credit. Ray had our mother's beautiful ocean blue eyes. He looked like a young George Bush. He has cirrhosis of the liver now, from drinking.

I wish desperately that I'd known back then what a lack of motherly love and attention do to a child. When we'd arrived on the bus from Arizona I was five, Joy was four, and Ray was two. I never remember seeing him held or picked up from then on. He always followed Joy and me, silently watching us, hands always in his overall pockets, never complaining. He only cried if we got too far ahead of him or he fell. There he'd lie, on his stomach, hands in pockets underneath, trapped until we'd run back for him. Like that little boy trapped on the ground unable to move because his hands were pocket-tied, Ray needed help he never got. His hands could have been freed. Through love, he could have learned to stand on his own two feet, but life kept tripping him up and love never reached him in time. Now it is too late.

Ray wasn't potty-trained when he came from Florida. Our stepmother set to in a hurry, for she wasn't going to be changing a big old two-year-old who pooped his pants. When he had an accident she pinned old tea dishtowels on him and made him stand outside for everyone to see him. When she saw anyone looking at him, she'd go out and explain, belittling him, making fun of him. She nailed him to his own private crucifix using nails of humiliation. There was not to be a resurrection for Ray, Daddy never stepped in. No one came to his rescue, and gradually those nails of humiliation turned into lifelong spikes that defied excision from a slashed soul. When he was about thirteen, Ray fell at the swimming pool. For three days he limped and dragged himself around by pulling on furniture. Finally they took him to the doctor. His hip was fractured. Even then he received no sympathy. My stepmother never stopped belittling him and downgrading him.

Once our real mother sent us a package. It had a pink dress and pinafore for me, a blue dress and pinafore for Joy, and nothing for little Ray. She never forgot that she nearly died at his birth. Somehow he was the scapegoat. It was his fault for being born, and besides, she had never wanted him anyway. Ray walked through life unwanted by the person who counts most in our early lives: a mother. No mother ever wanted him, and his big sister's love just wasn't enough to make up the loss. His real mother seemed determined to forget that he had even been born. His stepmother used his presence as a practice target to hone her skills of cruelty and humiliation.

All his life Ray longed for the mother he never got. A few years ago when he was living less than a hundred miles from his real mother, Ray called her, asking if he could see or write to her. She refused his request. It is hard to imagine a human doing that, but she managed. She didn't want to risk "getting hurt," she said. Poor little Ray.

Like this tangled tale of genes and genealogy, Daddy was a product of twists and turns of gene pools and genealogical happenstance, just as we all are. Although we were his own flesh and blood, he never interfered with the cruelties of our stepmother. She was free to do whatever she pleased with us. And so was he, being our natural father. Hers were more devious. His were more direct. Humiliation from her; beatings from him. One, emotional abuse. The other, physical abuse. She ignored his cruelties to us. Sexual improprieties and abuses were overlooked. Beatings were never interfered with.

Their capacity for accepting the evil in one another worked to their benefit and our damage. Even though he produced damaged goods, he was still the manufacturer. He was our only daddy. Apparently that gave him rights without limits.

His shortcomings were sometimes cloaked with layers of intelligence. Perhaps it was his very brilliance that helped damage him, for we now know that madness and genius often have the capacity to dwell side by side. Then again, brilliance can leave a person behind socially because he is so far ahead intellectually. That is the story of too many of us: the irony of being behind because we are ahead. There are more ways of being ahead than just intellect. Talent, drive, motivation, energy, physical abilities—the list stretches endlessly, and so do the memories of exclusion by those who excel. The big question is how we handle those excellent places within us. Do we become defeated over exclusion or determined to win through excelling? Discouraged or determined? Therein lies the difference.

Chapter Twenty-One

THE RANGE RIDER

I was nine and in fourth grade when the Range Rider event happened. Different children had been having birthday parties throughout the year, and I had gone to some of them. We played things like pin the tail on the donkey, musical chairs, or team games, things like fish or pit. After the games, there was ice cream and cake and soda pop. Most of the parties had balloons, and some even had hats! The gifts were all piled up, and after the ice cream and cake, the birthday person got to unwrap them in front of us all. Sometimes there was music. Always it was fun!

Easter was over, school would close in just nine more weeks, and my mid-May birthday would soon be coming up. Although I'd gone to some, I'd never had a birthday party. In my innocence I thought that if I kept it easy and inexpensive, maybe my stepmother would finally let me have one.

I thought about it a lot before I brought the subject up to my stepmother. I guess fantasy got mixed up with hope, because I finally dared to ask her.

"Mama, could I invite some of my friends over for my birthday?" I asked, expecting a curt refusal.

"Don't see why not, if it's just for Jell-O."

Hearing twisted its way into my ears. I doubted what I'd heard. "Oh, Ma! Do you really mean it? How wonderful! I know they'd love Jell-O. I bet they like strawberry, don't you, Mama? Oooh, Mama, do you s'pose I could invite the Range Rider to come too, Ma? Do you s'pose he'd come?" My voice spiraled higher and higher as my ecstasy and excitement grew.

Every day when school was out I would rush home and watch *Dick West and the Range Rider* on the television set. He was the man we know today as "Walker," and I knew he lived at that time in Phoenix, right next door to Tempe. He was my hero. A good man who always caught the bad fellow, he stood for what was right. The Range Rider was my idol, the hero who could rescue people who needed help. Besides that he was a kind person, I could tell! And he lived nearby!

"Do you think he'd come, Mama?" I repeated.

"Oh, Jeanne!" she muttered, not looking up, but then she stopped talking for a minute. Suddenly she lifted her head and looked at me. "Ah—I'm sure he'd just love to come to your birthday party," she said with a strange little smile. "In fact, you don't even have to invite him. I'll write and ask him myself!"

I couldn't believe this miracle of kindness being given me. Each day I would skip home from school with a happy little smile in my heart, rush into the house, and breathlessly ask if Ma had heard from the Range Rider yet. Finally one day she said yes, she had heard, and he said he would come. When I asked to see the letter she said she had already burned it up in the trash. I really felt bad about that. I could have taken it to school and showed all the kids. The boys might even have wanted to trade me something for his signature, but I knew I'd never want to give or trade away a letter from him. I didn't understand why Stepmother would throw such an important letter away, but I allowed my disappointment to be buried under the excitement that Range Rider was really coming to my birthday party! Mine! I could hardly wait for the sun to bubble up through the black, star-pricked Arizona sky so I could go to school and tell everyone that the Range Rider was coming to my house! He really was! He was coming to Tempe to our very own house!

I was too excited to eat breakfast and even had trouble dressing. I was trying to go too fast so I could get off to school and have time before classes to tell everyone. I had to go back from the kitchen and change socks because they didn't match, but finally I was on my way, rushing out the door, shouting good-bye to an unresponsive environment. No matter. No matter at all. Nothing could be wrong with this day!

I bounced effortlessly to school that day and rushed onto the school yard exclaiming, "Guess what!" to all my friends. "I'm having a birthday party, and you'll never guess who is coming to it! The Range Rider!" I was instantly the most popular girl in class.

From that day on I thought incessantly about my birthday. The list of those invited got longer. At first I just invited the ones who had me to their birthday parties, but I was so excited about having the Range Rider there that I finally had included the class. The whole class. Everyone in it! *But not any other classes,* I told myself, *so it probably will be okay.* Nevertheless, I started worrying about whether StepMother would be mad because I had invited so many. Since I never knew what would set off her wrath I delayed telling her. After all, this was the first birthday party I'd ever had, and I didn't want her anger to spoil it.

Finally, it was the day before the party, and I knew I had to give her an idea of how many were coming. She didn't like surprises, and I didn't want her to be surprised and get mad at me and maybe call off the party. She'd do it if she felt like it, I knew, and my friends and I at school had been able to talk of nothing else for weeks. It was the most exciting thing to happen to us all in the whole year! The boys even quit teasing us girls as much and treated me especially with great respect. They loved the Range Rider!

"Aw, the Range Rider ain't comin' to your house," some of them scoffed, half teasing and half wanting reassurance that it was all for real.

"He is too! Just ask my mama! She said so, and she even wrote and invited him and he answered and said yes! You'll see!" I said in total belief.

The day before the party however, I began to get butterflies in my stomach. I dragged home from school slowly, worried about Stepmother's reaction when I told her how many kids I had invited. More and more I regretted inviting so many, but it was so exciting to have the Range Rider come, and all the kids envied me so much I couldn't help it. I'd just had to ask them all.

"Mama," I said as soon as I entered the door, "I've invited twenty-three kids to the party tomorrow. I hope that's not too many. The whole class wanted to come when they heard the Range Rider was going to be here. I'll make the Jell-O myself," I volunteered, hoping this would offset any anger.

My stepmother turned to look at me, snorted, and then with lips curled, snarled, "Why you little fool, you! Did you really think I would invite the Range Rider to come to your birthday party? He'd never come for someone like you, you skinny, stupid little brat. Don't you know *anything?* Besides, there ain't going to be any birthday party. We don't have money to spend on any party, and especially for you, you dunce!"

The next day I went to school and told my classmates that I couldn't have my birthday party. That is how I came to be known to the fourth-grade teacher and to all my classmates as a liar.

I never explained to anyone.

What was the use?

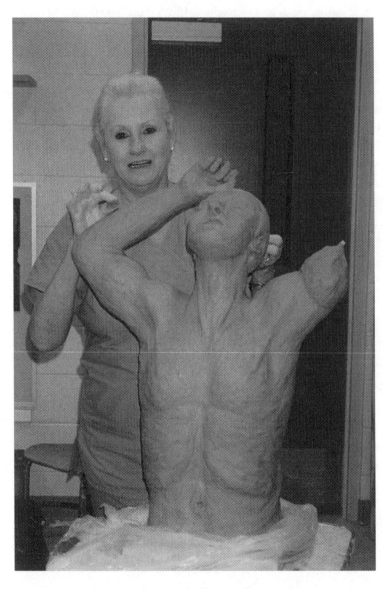

Adam's exile from Eden

Displaying "Michael" and "Earth Weeps"

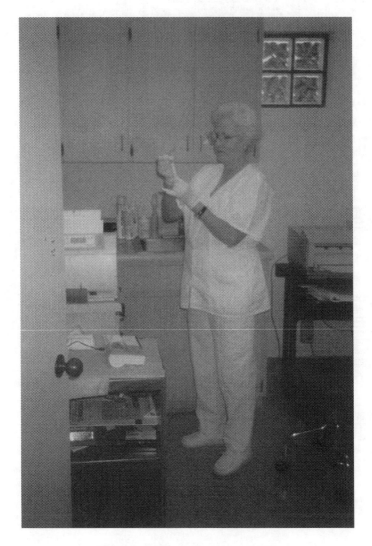

Testing a patient. Jeanne at work

"The Blessing"

"Ashley"

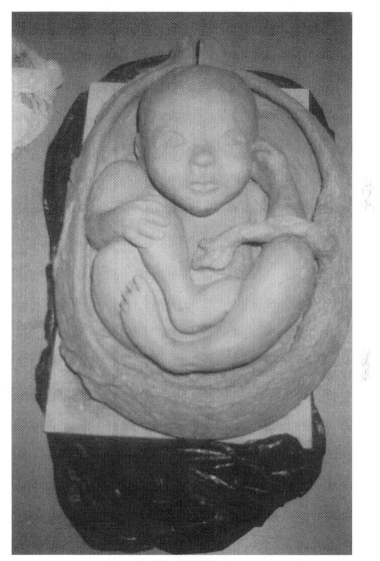

"Chandler"

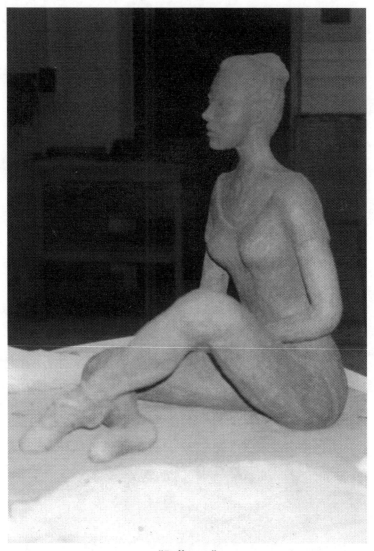

"Ballerina"

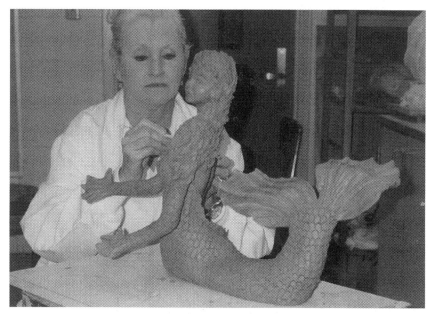

"Mermaid"

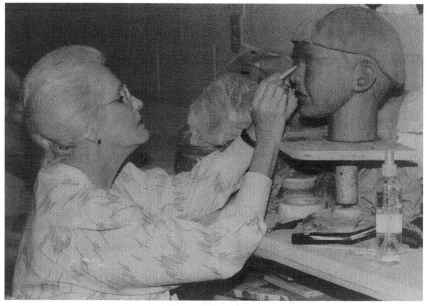

"Joshua"

Chapter Twenty-Two

<u>LITTLE LIAR?</u>

As a youngster I had seen and experienced too much in my home; there was too much I could tell. Even though I knew that Aunt Nell had believed me, my concept of adults changed as time inched on. I no longer looked to any of them with hope. There was no one out there for me, for everyone I met would think I was a bad girl, a liar, an unfit companion for their children, their family, or themselves, according to my stepmother. She tried to ingrain in me that idea, because she was so afraid that I would tell someone about our home situation.

When I was seven and living in the tobacco barn, I told a neighbor about our family. When Stepmother found out she beat me horribly and told me that "what goes on in this house stays in this house." To her face I called her Mama, because she told me to and I was too frightened a child to disobey. However, she was never anything but "Stepmother" in my heart … forever, because she always made sure that everyone knew Joy, Ray, and I weren't her children. How could she deny us in one breath and tell us to call her "Mama" in another?

Hope dies slowly in a child's heart, but hope, for me, had already begun to splinter by the time I was six or seven. Too early. Such early disillusionment can only cause twisted, fragmented splinters in the psyche.

In the fifth grade I went to school one day after experiencing one of my beatings the previous evening. My legs were covered with red welts and fresh scabs from where the razor strap had cut into my flesh enough to make me bleed. I had a ratty old hairbrush, but it was mine, and I took it to school each day so I could try and make myself look right. Miss Trestler called me over when the kids were going out to recess. "Jeanne, may I borrow your brush?" I handed it over with shame, and she used it to brush her hair a few moments before asking if she could brush mine. As the brush stroked through my hair she made a statement I was never to forget. "What pretty hair you have!" she said. "It's so soft it's just like silk." It was the first compliment I remember ever receiving. I was stunned. I had never known that I had anything nice about me! Could it be true?

Those kind words we occasionally take time to speak—do they really matter? Never doubt it! Decades later I still consider my hair to be my crowning glory. It is the part of myself I give the most attention to and the first thing that people notice about me because of its "upsweep and color." "When I'm looking for you in a department store," one friend of mine noted, "I just look for an ash-blonde torch with hair high-piled, and when I see the glow, I know where you are."

"Jeanne, what is wrong with the back of your legs?" Miss Trestler splintered my reverie.

"Oh, that's just where Daddy hit me." I had spoken before I thought. Would I get another beating? Would she tell what I had said? My fourth-grade teacher came in to the room to visit Miss Trestler during recess break. They talked softly together as Miss Trestler continued to stroke my hair. "This should be reported!" she said and motioned toward my legs.

"Honey, you're young and haven't been teaching long," the veteran teacher whispered. "You think about this before you do it, because it means you'll have to go to court 'n face the parents 'n have your name in the paper. Besides, it could drag on fo' months. Do y'all really want that much of a mess?"

"But this is so wrong!" Miss Trestler demurred.

"Well, I hate to see you git in a mess yoah first year here, so ah'm goin to tell you: I know fer a fact this child is a liar. Last year she lied to the whole class about the Ranger Rider comin' to her birthday party. Then at the last minute she called off the party with no explanation."

Miss Trestler never singled me out after that and never had much time for me. I learned another lesson that year: don't hope. Don't ever let your heart lift expectantly. You're never too young to learn: don't trust Big People. It's a good lesson to learn.

Chapter Twenty-Three

RANSOMED BIRD; BOY AFIRE!

While we were back in the old house in Tempe, I went through the sixth to eighth grade. I had never gone to school in one so place for so long before. When I was eleven, I was playing in our backyard in an old abandoned car, pretending it was my house, decorating it with junk, and alternately pretending to drive to the store. I always played alone now. Little John, now five, was playing around out there too, but we weren't playing together. The other kids were off about somewhere. In the yard smoldered a big metal barrel that was used for burning trash. Little John was highly intelligent and inquisitive. He also played alone.

Suddenly I saw John carrying a big red kerosene can that I knew was about half full. He was headed for the smoldering trash can. Screaming, "No, John! No John!" I raced toward him. He reached the trash can first. Holding the spout in his left arm and the handle in his right, he leaned over the open can and splashed kerosene in. Flames shot up high into the air, catching fire in his hair and eyebrows. His left arm was a blaze of fire, as he'd evidently splashed it on him when he was playing earlier. I grabbed him and began beating the fire out with my hands. My screams for help mingled with his screams of pain. With the fire out on him I grabbed him up with a strength that wasn't mine and ran for the house.

My stepmother came to see what was going on. I yelled to get ice, and she said, "No, get butter." John's snow-white head ("Cottontop," as my stepmother called him) was singed. His eyebrows and eyelashes were singed, but worse was the right arm. My stepmother sent me into the house for butter. We had an old cow, so we had butter, but I came back with ice and told her the school nurse said always put ice on burns to stop the burning and scarring. She didn't take time to argue with me; we just did it.

It was years before I learned that neither treatment was right. Ice damages the scored skin and butter keeps air from it, rubs salt in it, and adds to the danger of infection. Then my stepmother sent me for a bottle of rubbing alcohol and some of Daddy's clean handkerchiefs. We made a bandage for John's arm and she poured alcohol down it. She jumped in the old pickup truck with John to take him to the doctor, instructing me to "stay there and watch for the other kids." Then she was gone in a cloud of dust and anxiety.

I stuck my blistered hands on what was left of the ice and waited. When they got home little John's arm was a sheath of bandages, gauze, and tape. As soon as Daddy came home she told him that John was burned with the kerosene. Because I'd been outside when John was, he thought I should have known what he was doing.

He took off his belt and came for me, but my stepmother stopped him and said, "No! She saved him! The doctor said that judging by the way he was burned and what he'd done, he would have been killed if she hadn't been right there and acted so quickly."

Daddy looked at me and stepped back. His arm dropped. That night, I didn't get a whipping. Once again, Stepmother had intervened for me. It was one of those occasions when she supported me. I never forgot those times; they were very rare but always so welcome!

Miraculously little John's hair came back, his eyebrows grew out, and he had no scars. My own miracle was smaller but was just as real to me. I didn't receive a beating! I was given neither credit nor thanks for helping John, but at least I wasn't beaten. That was a miracle to me. Another miracle that year was the start of my love for nursing. It all began because I had nothing for lunch.

I was eleven that day in Tempe when there was nothing for me to fix my lunch with—no mayonnaise, no bread, nothing. Stepmother gave Gil, Lee, Dolly, and John money to buy lunch tickets, as she did every day. Joy and Ray always got what I got: two pieces of bread with some mayonnaise spread between. They had already had their lunch and were gone when Stepmother said to me, "I forgot your lunch." How could she remember six lunches and forget mine? But maybe it was easy since four of them always got money and she had to remember to have mayonnaise and bread for us. You'd think it would be easy to remember, but this time she hadn't enough on hand for all three of us, and I was last in line.

I don't know why we didn't get school lunch money like the other kids. Or maybe I didn't want to know. It told me too much about how she felt about us and how she thought we fit into the scheme of being considered human. She gave me twelve cents, which was "all she had," and I was to "buy milk with it" (Milk always made me vomit, as I'm lactose intolerant) "and buy a roll or something with what's left," she'd add indifferently.

When lunchtime came I lingered behind so I would be last in the line. I was ashamed that I couldn't buy a regular thirty-five-cent lunch and afraid to ask the lunch ladies what I could get for twelve cents. As I walked across the field toward the lunch room I saw three boys kneeling on the ground looking at something. One held a rock in his hand. As I approached I saw that it was a baby bird, all bare pink flesh, stomach bulging, not a feather to its name. I knelt beside them.

"Let me go ahead and kill it," the boy with the rock said to the others.

"Oh, please don't! Let me have it; I'll take care of it!" I intervened. "What happened to his feathers?" I said, hoping to divert them.

They said they'd pulled them out. Noticing the nest in the tree on the old schoolyard that the bird had fallen from and not knowing that some baby birds hatch out like that, I believed them and began to sob.

"Please, please let me have him!" I cried.

"What will you give us?"

All I had was the twelve cents my stepmother had given me to buy a partial lunch. I opened my clutched fist and held it out to them.

"That's all you've got? I'm just going to go ahead and kill him."

"No!" I sobbed. "Please!" After more tear-wet pleas they took my meager lunch money and raced to the nearly finished cafeteria line, where they'd been headed when the bird fell from the nest.

I carried the pitiful bundle of pin feathers and weak chirps back to my classroom and knelt on the floor of the coatroom amid lockers and coat hooks. All I had to give him were sips of water. Kids were returning from the lunch room. I begged them for any crumbs they had. Of course there were few crumbs, but a lot of interest. Just then Teacher came to see what all the commotion was. As I held him, sobbing, she made me tell her the story. Then she sent a child to the principal's office to summon him.

It wasn't long before Mr. Holman strode in, glasses winking, wearing a concerned frown on his face. He questioned me and the teacher and then excused me from class to go with him. He assured me that I could leave the bird with the teacher, who promised to watch it until I got back. Together, we went to the lunch room where he had me identify the three boys who were torturing the baby bird. Once again I was dismissed.

As I was going out one of the boys yelled he was going to get me good, but Mr. Holman grabbed him and told him he'd better never touch me. He took the boys to the office, where they all got whipped. You'd think they would have been out to get me after that, but none of them ever tried to touch me. I lived in fear for some time, though.

After I returned to class and was assured that the bird was being properly tended and that I could take it home with me that night, I accepted the note that teacher told me to carry to the lunch room. It was a note telling them to feed me. They were cleaning up but nevertheless managed to unearth some food and make me eat; however, I was so worried about the little bird that every passing moment stuck in my throat along with the food I was struggling to swallow. All I wanted was to get back to the classroom.

I rush-returned to class, now in session. I was late, but the teacher said it was okay since she'd sent me. All afternoon the teacher repeatedly warned us to "get back to work" as we all struggled to keep our curiosity lidded. Occasional cheeps fed the fires of our curiosity.

Something unexpected came out of the bird episode, however. The next day the school nurse came and called me out of class and took me to her office, where she examined me and asked lots of questions—how many kids in our family, their names, grades, etc. Evidently the principal had talked to her. They checked on everything I told them. It was on their records that Lee and Gil and Dolly and John always had lunch tickets, but never Joy or Ray or me. She weighed and measured me. There was a long silence. Finally she asked me if I'd like to work in the nurse's office at recess and after lunch each day rolling bandages, answering phones, and cleaning and bandaging minor wounds if the nurse was out. In return for my work I'd get a daily lunch ticket. From then on I worked in the nurse's office every day at recess in order to earn my lunch. The nurse ran errands while I took messages and "rolled bandages." These were long torn sheet strips, rolled endlessly until gone. I checked kids in and put Band-Aids on them. For two years every day while the other children played, I worked … and loved it! As I worked there, the nurse taught me basic practical medicine. We kept track of the height and weight of all the kids in school. Because of my small weight and size they kept a close watch over me. In the sixth grade I finally hit fifty pounds!

It wasn't long after I began working in the nurse's office that Joy and Ray were also "weighed and found lacking." My sister Joy was enlisted to work in the school lunch room, cleaning tables to help earn her lunch. Ray too was given chores to earn his lunch tickets. Funny how some folks can be aware of the need to preserve one's pride, even at tender ages. Not only that, but we had been given dignity by being chosen to help in the cafeteria and a nurse's room! Self-esteem, like a kite, was rising on the winds of acceptance and approval.

A few days before all this, Ray's teacher sent a note home reporting that Ray slept at school most of the day and that she had to wake him up. "Would Daddy please talk to him and see he gets proper rest?" Daddy talked to him all right. He beat him with the razor strap and made him go to bed at 7:30 every night. Authorities never knew about Ray's beatings, but after the school nurse started weighing and checking on us she discovered that poor Ray's eyes were so bad he couldn't even see the blackboard. He got thick glasses. By this time he was in the third grade and had had an untreated eye problem called amblyopia for years. Later Joy got glasses also.

A profound influence had invaded my life! Nursing came to mean compassion, concern, caring, and healing to me. These became my focus in life. My goal was to be a nurse. I wanted nothing else. That was my driving force throughout the following years. Even though I wasn't able to go to nursing school long enough to get a nursing degree after graduation, I still managed to enter the field of medicine, eventually becoming a skilled phlebotomist and medical assistant. I trace my love for the medical field directly to a compassionate nurse, principal, and teacher, back in those years of baby birds and bad boys.

It was the only school we ever went to where teachers cared enough to check into our living arrangements and to notice our physical conditions. What a difference an observant teacher or neighbor can make in a child's life!

The day after I ransomed the bird and took it home I went to school as usual. When I got home that night the bird was dead. "It just died," my stepmother said. It still lives on in my memory, because it began a change for me that gave my life direction.

Chapter Twenty-Four

CHASING PICKUPS

Our move to Tempe, Arizona, gave me the first opportunity of my life to go to school with the same class for more than one year. We lived in Tempe for three years, the longest I remembered living anywhere. Finally there was time to get acquainted with classmates. From that gift of time grew a fast friendship with Gwen, my first best friend.

Gwen and I got into all sorts of things together, from exploring the possibility of starting a newspaper to dressing up as ballerinas: two skinny little kids, dancing in the Arizona fields with dust balls and tumbleweed. Even abused children are not sad all the time, and I was becoming more and more determined to find humor in any situation it could be plucked from. If I was as "skinny as a chicken" and "stupid as a goose," then, by golly, I was going to learn how to pluck feathers of fun and humor, making my cage a henhouse of happiness. I would live up to my chicken appellation in an unexpected way.

By the time I was ten, nearly eleven, I finally passed the fifty-pound weight mark. I was indeed a bit of a skinny chick. Skinny or not, I was a chick—a female—and this seemed to become more and more apparent to my father's eye. I had learned way back at the age of four to avoid his roaming hands and to fear being alone with him. Without fully understanding my uneasiness, I knew that something was wrong with the situations he began putting me in more and more. I was afraid of him. This caused me to try avoidance rather than courage or confrontation. If I told someone else, he would just lie. I tried that once, and I was the one to be punished. There was no escape. A child is dominated by the adults in her life, who will say she has little credibility or label her "highly imaginative."

No escape. No escape! Do you know what *no escape* is like? Imagine yourself being swaddled in soft cloth, arms at your side, until you are incapable of moving. Imagine trying to scream only to have silence strangle your shouts. Imagine being totally helpless, without credibility, without strength, without wisdom, without weapons. No. Way. Out. Trapped.

When I was in the sixth grade one day I went into the house to the bathroom. Gwen and I had been playing outside. She left to go home. I knew Daddy was in the house, but so was the rest of the family, so I had nothing to fear. Suddenly, I heard the engine on our old pickup start. Was Daddy going somewhere, or was it Stepmother, going shopping? I burst out of the bathroom and ran to the window in time to see everyone but my father piling into the pickup.

Frantically, I ran outside hoping to catch the old truck before it hit the highway. It had already started moving, but there was a shortcut that would help: I ran across a big field to cut off distance. I knew my stepmother was going to the grocery store, and I dared not be left home alone. It wasn't safe. But none of them knew that. Who would have believed me if they had known? Who would have cared?

All the kids except me were in the truck. Had Stepmother left me alone with Daddy deliberately? My stepbrother Gil was in the back of the truck by the tailgate. Gil was six months younger than me but already much taller and bigger. As I ran, flapping my skinny arms, I was screaming and yelling, "Wait! Wait!" I knew they couldn't help but see me. Certainly Gil did.

I neared the highway from the big field, closing up the distance. I could hear Gil yell, "Speed up, Mama. Speed up," so she did. Gil knelt in the back laughing and pointing a finger at me.

Suddenly, Stepmother slowed down. It wasn't until later that I realized that she had seen me in the rearview mirror and was slowing to give me fresh hopes of catching up with the truck. When I was nearly there, she sped up again. I ran along the highway trying to catch up, falling behind and catching up again only to fall behind once more, with tears of terror rolling down my face.

My chest heaved with painful breaths, and a stitch in my side ached fiercely. I knew I mustn't get left behind. My feet pounded down the dusty road as I watched the truck alternate speeds. By now I'd run over a mile and a half, with Stepmother slowing down and then speeding up and Gil taunting me. Certainly she knew I was back there; this was her way of having fun. Later I learned that people along the highway had begun to watch the situation. The truck was moving so slowly, in order to keep me running, that it attracted attention. Window watchers and front-yard and porch-sitting folks were drawn to the spectacle. They could hear me screaming and see me crying. Suddenly the old pickup pulled over and stopped.

Gratefully, I pulled my skinny little legs over the tailgate and fell into the back of the truck. As I was climbing in, Gil said, "Aw, Mom, why'd you stop for her?" Right then, coming from the other direction, a police car passed, and I knew why my stepmother had stopped for me. It was not out of pity or concern. She had seen the approaching police car.

"Why Jeanne," she sneered, "I didn't see you back there until just this minute! Why didn't you let us know you wanted to go to town?" I was too winded, too exhausted, and too worried to answer. Oh, I knew she knew, but what could I say? Again, I was helpless, but I would choose this sort of helplessness over the kind I felt with my Daddy.

I'd fallen into the floor of the truck, feeling the hard metal with its uneven ridges beneath my face. The cool evening air blew on my now soaking wet clothes. My skinny arms and legs were ice cold now, and my head swirled with dizziness. In a few minutes more the truck came to the edge of town and rolled toward the supermarket looking like any average family taking the kids out for a ride and a treat. Everyone piled out with shouts of joy. Almost everyone. "You stay right there," my stepmother hissed, looking straight at me. We three were never allowed to go into the store with the rest of the family. As usual we sat outside in the back of the truck by ourselves, without any treat like the others would get, but I didn't care. I had managed to escape, and that was all that mattered.

Gradually my heart thuds slowed down and I was able to breathe without gasping. I have no idea how much time passed before the others came out with treats in their hand; I only knew I had been saved from an alternative I didn't even care to think about. But now I had to begin thinking about what awaited me upon our return home.

When we got to the house, Daddy was waiting inside. He looked huge and menacing as he stood half in and half out of evening shadows that were clawing their way inside the house. Stepmother told him how I had chased the truck and she'd tried to "teach her a lesson by making her run it out for nearly two miles." It was nearly dark by then, but none of us had yet had supper. Daddy looked at me with a glitter in his eyes and said he ought to whip me with his belt but he'd let me off this time; however, I must go to bed with no supper.

Gratefully, I said, "Yes, sir," and went shaky-happy into the bedroom to put on my old flannel nightgown. I crawled into the bed I shared with my sister Joy. My head spun for a while, and my bony body shook with fear. Finally I fell asleep. After a couple of hours my sister Joy came to bed. She woke me with a whisper. She'd washed the dishes and smuggled me out a piece of bread with butter and said it was all she could get. I plunged my head under the covers and gobbled it down, overly grateful for these crumbs of kindness. It was the most compassionate thing I can remember Joy doing for me in her young life. As she matured, she was diagnosed as having an "attachment disorder." No wonder. How can unloved children learn to love others? Their lives are rudderless.

Crumbs of compassion were few and far between ... from anyone, for any of the three of us.

Chapter Twenty-Five

HOUSE AFIRE!

Sometimes it takes years to learn truths about ourselves; truths we should have learned as children. People used to think you shouldn't compliment children; it would make them vain. Doubtless my "family" never even got that far in thinking about me. I was not regarded as someone who might need reassurance and encouragement. I doubt I was even thought of as totally human. Thus, it would never have occurred to them to suggest that I had attractive features or wasn't truly stupid, as I so often heard.

I grew up believing I was both stupid and sorry-looking. I made good grades, but my stepmother told me it was only because the teachers felt sorry for me. I could work on my looks, however, so I became a meticulous dresser, careful about my cleanliness, grooming, makeup, and dress. People kept telling me I was pretty as I got older, but I didn't believe it. I had been told from an early age how ugly I was. Strange how our very own eyes cannot see truth if we have repeatedly been taught contrary to what we see.

It was not until I was in my fifties that my best friend, a teacher, began repeatedly showing me examples of intelligence I exhibited. Even then it was some time before I began to believe her.

"I always thought I was stupid," I murmured. "All the children are exceptional, but I just figured they had very intelligent fathers."

It was hard to believe that I might not be stupid after all. Eventually I remembered a childhood event that illustrated some signs of intelligence that helped me begin to believe in my own self-worth.

Gwen was my best friend in those preteen years. We had much in common, even though she was a year younger than me, a big difference at that age! Her mother had been given to a thirty-six-year-old man, Fred Martin, when she was twelve. The day following their marriage he told her to get up and shave him.

She laughed and said, "Get up and shave yourself, you lazy bum!"

He got up all right—to get his belt and beat her severely. She never disobeyed an order again. In little more than a dozen years they had nine children. He continued his violent assaults on her and the children, but paralyzed by fear, she could never bring herself to try to escape. Some years later, with five children now gone, he beat her twelve-year-old son unconscious. She had been beaten many times trying to protect the children, but this time Freddy Jr. had been trying to protect her.

That was the day Gwen's mother-in-law, having followed this saga of grief for longer than she could endure, finally called the sheriff. Quietly, the law set about relocating Mrs. Martin and her three children to a safe place in the country. That's how Gwen came to live within walking distance of our family.

They didn't have much, a few pieces of furniture and, once Mrs. Martin got work at a local factory, an old car, but they were safe and happy until one day old Fred Martin saw her leaving work and followed her. She didn't think anything about it when she heard the knock on the door. At first he was polite, saying he had just come to visit the kids. Once inside however, he beat and raped her.

This time he was put into jail for several years, but it was too late for her—she was already pregnant again. The factory where she worked helped a lot by taking up contributions for her. She kept the towheaded little baby girl, Jennifer, who became a playmate to my towheaded brother John, eight years my junior. Sometimes I would take him with me to play with her, but if I could, I would sneak off without him because once he tired and I took him home, Stepmother wouldn't let me back out the rest of the day if she thought I was having fun.

We played "restaurant" or "garden" all morning, drawing pictures in the hard dirt of the plants we were "growing" in our garden. At lunch time, when Mrs. Martin called Gwen in, I would go down the street to hide in some bushes, waiting for Gwen to reemerge, usually with some hidden morsel for me to eat. If I went home I wouldn't be allowed to return. If I had to go to the bathroom, I used the bushes, since Stepmother said I wasn't allowed to use other people's toilets.

Gwen and I shared our dreams and hopes. For years I had fantasized about being a great ballerina. I learned to walk barefoot on the tips of my bare feet. I checked out books from the school library, drawing pictures of each position, learning them by heart until I was "just perfect" in Gwen's opinion. I didn't know what you did after you were in position, but I got the positions down pat, balancing in some gargoyle-ish pose like a frozen, slightly wobbly ice statue. Gwen and I practiced diligently, leaping around open lawns and the weed-strewn field on spindly little chicken legs, dust puffing up from our feet, twirling and dancing to music only we could hear.

Dusk was beginning to nip at the edges of our idyllic day, and I knew I would get a whipping if I didn't get home soon. I traveled a bit slower that week because of a toe infected by a big sticker. It was wrapped in a rag with a piece of bacon fat in it to draw the poison out and meant I had to wear shoes, which I hated. The best shoes I ever wore were "barefoot." Still are.

Shadows were knitting the eight-foot oleander bush together as I passed Jack and Betty's old deserted house. A few weeks before we moved in they had advertised all their old furniture for sale, gave the few remaining sticks away, and proclaimed the house for sale. Daddy went down and inquired about the price of the old stucco structure. He laughingly said they must think they had a gold mine there; no one in his right mind was going to pay that. Daddy ordered us never to play on their property, so I began to pass the old deserted house without another thought. I knew those oleander bushes well, though; this is where I hid while waiting for Gwen to eat lunch and where I went when I needed a bathroom. You had to put your shoes on to get in them, however; they would tear your feet up otherwise.

Suddenly I spotted Mr. Jack. He was just getting out of a nice new-looking beige car, different from his usual one. He hadn't seen me. He was alone. I was afraid. Mr. Jack always cussed us kids if he saw us outside. Twilight had called everyone in, and rather than walk across the front of the house and be seen, I crawled into my hiding place. By then I had learned to fear men, and Mr. Jack seemed especially mean. He looked up and down the empty road and opened the trunk.

He took out a big red can with a spout, just like the one John got burned with, the same as Daddy had in his shop. He walked across the street with it, leaning a bit to one side.

As he approached the gate a car came rattling down the street, and he quickly stepped inside the gate and stood motionless beside the hedge. As soon as the car passed he began pouring what looked like water all over the yard. I wondered why he didn't use a hose to water his lawn. He went all around the house with it.

Suddenly, when he came within about three feet of my hiding place, he tensed up as if he had sensed or heard something. I dared not breathe so the bushes wouldn't move. Just then, about eight feet from me, there was a rattle in the bushes and an old cat leaped out and ran. Mr. Jack grabbed a big gray rock from the side of the walkway and hit the old cat broadside. The cat fell and then staggered up and ran off. Mr. Jack smiled as though he enjoyed hitting the cat, which made me tremble even more.

He picked up his can and went in the front door. I was afraid to move for fear he would come out at any moment. Finally he emerged carrying the can he now swung so easily at his side. He looked up and down the empty street again and went to the car, opened the trunk, put the can in, turned on his headlights, and left.

As soon as he was gone I made a dash for home. Even though it wasn't completely dark yet, it was rapidly approaching. Daddy caught me trying to slip in undetected. He had his razor strap in hand. I told him about Mr. Jack and why I was late. But he didn't care why, and I got a whipping.

Later that night we were awakened by the sound of sirens. Fire trucks seemed everywhere. Mr. Jack's house was ablaze! Some of the oleander bushes were on fire. Oleander emits a poisonous gas on burning, so we couldn't play outdoors for a couple of days. I heard Daddy tell Stepmother that he thought someone had torched the old house and it was probably a case of arson. I didn't know what arson was, but I couldn't wait to get to my friend Gwen's to play and talk about the fire.

Two days later I was finally allowed to go out. As I approached the Jack house on the way, Mr. Jack and Mrs. Betty and some other people were standing around the yard.

"Come over here!" Mr. Jack yelled. I just knew he had seen me that night and was going to maybe even beat me for hiding on his property. I was afraid, but Mrs. Betty smiled at me as if she would protect me, so I timidly ventured closer.

"Hey kid, the police suspect arson with this here old house." (There was that word again.) "You kids haven't been playing over here, have you?"

I put my hands on my hips and indignantly said, "You know our daddy won't let us play over here. Besides, the last person I saw here was you, two nights ago when you came with the red can to water your lawn and wash inside your house." Mr. Jack turned beet red and snarled, "You little liar; you get out of here! I wasn't anywhere near here!" I ran on to Gwen's and forgot about it. Big people were always yelling at me; this was just more of the same.

A few days later I was on my way home and there in the yard with Daddy was one of the men who had been standing with Mr. Jack and Mrs. Betty in their yard. Daddy said, "Jeanne, I want you to tell me again what you got a whipping over." So I told him the story all over again. I explained everything about the red can and the new car and its color and said I didn't know he had a new car. I didn't know car makes or models so couldn't answer the man's questions, but I had a habit of memorizing car license tags. Don't ask me why; I just did it for fun, I guess.

"I can't tell you anything else about the car except its color and the license tag number," I said.

There was a long pause and then, "What did you say?" from the insurance man.

I repeated it and tacked on the license number, which I still remembered, for good measure. He looked at Daddy and then went away, shaking his head.

We never saw Mr. Jack or Mrs. Betty again. Daddy never told me how I had helped solve the crime. He never praised me, never mentioned my memory or how my observance had solved a crime. Things went on as usual, and I remained the same stupid, ugly girl I'd always been. I continued to believe that for another forty-some years.

Chapter Twenty-Six

ONE PARTICULAR DAY

One afternoon when I was about twelve, I came home from school planning to go outside to play, escaping the house as quickly as possible. "Home" was an ugly word, a place to fear and avoid. Home is where you took a lot of hits, both verbal and physical. The emotional ones were the worst, though, just like this one particular day, which lives forever in my memory.

When I approached the house it was still and quiet inside. I was never comfortable with quietness in my father's house; the stillness always seemed thick and threatening. Corners felt menacing, as if some demon might jump out unexpectedly to confront me. I entered the sinister-seeming house and went quietly toward the bathroom, which was, ominously, in my father and stepmother's room. On the other side of the bathroom wall was the kitchen. As I rounded the doorway my heart froze. There lay Daddy on the bed taking a nap, but he was awake and dressed only in his underwear! I started to run too late. In a flash he was up and reaching for me. He grabbed my arm and began kissing me.

I started shouting, "I have to go to the bathroom. I have to use the bathroom!" There was no escape from the bathroom, as he knew, and I would have to reenter the bedroom.

"Go," he growled, "and then get right back out here."

I darted in, put the latch on the door, and turned to the outside wall where there was a window. Desperately I tried to open it. I couldn't hammer at it for fear Daddy would hear, but I pushed and tugged with all my might. It wouldn't budge; it had been painted shut years ago, and my twig-thin preadolescent arms lacked strength to break the paint bond. I felt like that window; trapped in place. The only door was the one I'd come in through. The old house we were living in was put together from pieces of other old houses. Where the old kitchen and bathroom joined the addition, there was a small pass-through about twelve inches big. It was left over from something else and was located above the bathtub, about three or four feet off the ground. I climbed onto the edge of the old claw-footed bathtub and shinnied my skinny little body through.

Daddy was outside yelling at me to get out of the bathroom. He began pounding on the door. It rattled and shook as if it would break. Frantically I put my head into the opening, arms first. My heart thudded like thunder in my ears. Desperately I wiggled and pushed. I could feel flesh peeling from my hips, pressure from the window frame bruising my arms. Suddenly I fell, headfirst, out the little opening onto the kitchen floor. Daddy heard the sound of me falling and knew what I had done. I could hear him rushing from the bedroom, feet pounding closer and closer. I ran for the kitchen, but he was already blocking that exit. I turned around and ran through the house, Daddy yelling at me, "Get back here!"

I fled out the back door as fast as my toothpick legs could carry me and ran toward the big field. Gwen's house was on the far side, but I knew she wasn't home.

Daddy followed, running after me and shouting. He saw me in the open field, but in his underwear he dared not follow. Just before Gwen's house there was an open drainage ditch. I reached it and dropped down, knowing that Daddy would think I was headed for Gwen's. I scuttled in the opposite direction, circling around toward Jack's old burned-out house. We weren't supposed to play in there because there were scorpions all over outside and nothing but rotting wood and burned pillars inside. The cinder blocks were deteriorating, and parts of the house could collapse at any time. Daddy couldn't find me, but I could peek out and see him standing in his underwear yelling.

He gave up then and went back into the house. I knew I'd better stay hidden until the old pickup came home. It seemed like I squatted inside in the darkness for hours, until finally I heard the old pickup come down the road. When the headlights shone, I ran, circling around so my hiding place wouldn't be known.

As the old truck pulled into the yard I arrived also, from the other way. There outside working in his "shop" was my daddy in his overalls, demanding to know where I'd been, as we were supposed to be in before dark.

"Please, please, please don't let me smell like smoke and burned wood," I begged someone. Getting out of the old pickup my stepmother demanded to know where I'd been.

White-faced and trembling I said, "I've been playing with Gwen and didn't notice it getting dark." What else could I say?

About that time my little brother Ray, who'd been in the back of the pickup, came back outside, loudly proclaiming that the bathroom door was locked inside and he needed to go. Everyone went inside, and Daddy had to pick up my little brother John, eight years my junior, and put him through the little pass-through to unlock the bathroom door. The next day Daddy nailed the pass-through shut.

Each blow of the hammer was a blowstrike of terror. Each nail put in place was a piercing death knell. There was no more escape.

Chapter Twenty-Seven

THE MOUSEVILLE EDITION

The season had swung into the rhythm of long, slow summer days; school-less days, with the sun striking like stabbing bladed from above; staying out in the solid sun to avoid going in and getting yelled at or struck unexpectedly for no reason. I guess I was a peculiar kid; I didn't much like summer. Little did I know that this was to be my last Arizona summer for a while.

My best friend Gwen and her two little sisters were going to their grandma's house for two weeks. Gwen was ecstatic. I was not. It was summertime, and I knew I'd be very lonesome with no one to play with. After Gwen was gone I moped around for a couple of days and then decided to explore the neighborhood. Each day, as soon as I had my work done, I took off. No one cared where I was as long as I didn't get into trouble. I was always real observant, curious, and careful to avoid trouble. As I explored, an idea began to germinate in my head.

As I said, I was a peculiar child, able to entertain myself endlessly, always looking for new and novel approaches to living. Thus it was that I decided to publish a newspaper. I would call it the "Mouseville Edition." Up and down our neighborhood from house to house I went, asking for any items people wanted to put in the news. I went to Ben Rowe and Layce Dean's house. She and Ben Rowe met when they were both cooks in a restaurant. Their house was always a "pigsty," my stepmother said, "piled high with junk." However, I'd found Layce Dean fun to talk to and to learn from. She'd showed me how to make real mayonnaise with eggs and oil. I copied her recipe for mayonnaise to print in my cooking section.

I moved on, down to Margaret Harris's house. Margaret and I were in the same grade at school, but she was a wanted child growing up in a loving, normal home. We had virtually nothing in common. Her grandmother, Mrs. Bannister, was there, and after I'd toured their rabbit hutches and allowed myself to accept the snack offered, I'd asked if they had any tidbits, recipes, or anything that was news.

Mrs. Bannister winked and told Margaret's mother, Mrs. Harris, that it was well known that "tall, dark, and handsome T. J. was seeing both L. K. of the horses and C. D. of the dogs while his wife stayed home and suffered."

That sounded like news to me. I didn't know any of the stars, but I figured it was movie talk.

"That's Hollywood for you," I thought as I faithfully wrote all the initials down, thanked them, and went on my way.

I made the rounds of everyone I could find and talked to everyone. At the far end of the road were the people who owned and raced greyhounds. They had six real wild kids beginning with the oldest, Cecelia, nineteen, all the way down to a newborn. I didn't like to go there because everything always smelled so "doggy."

At age twelve, I'd been sent there to baby-sit when the baby was only three weeks old. The oldest, Cecelia, was gone somewhere. Some of the kids were as big as I was, but I was considered a "good baby-sitter" and had the reputation of having "a good conscience." I think that meant I was honest and conscientious. The poor new baby cried and cried, and I'd held it, rocked it, and tried to give it its bottle while the other four jumped off furniture and fought. It was a madhouse and more than I knew how to handle. I told my stepmother never to send me there to baby-sit again. For some reason, she listened.

Well anyway, they gave me racing scores of races that their dogs had won. That would be good news in the paper. Up and down the road I went. One lady said she had a headache and not to bother her, so I went on my way. The lady at the other end of the road wasn't home, so I climbed across the ditch to investigate her golden palomino. He was beautiful but always had different girl horses coming to be pastured with him, and I considered his behavior totally inappropriate. He was a nasty-minded boy horse, I thought to myself.

Since the horse woman wasn't home and the headache lady didn't want to be bothered, I figured I had all the news on the street, so I hurried home to set up my newspaper. I got paper and pencils and began writing. I wrote and wrote, incorporating everything people had told or given me. At supper that night I jabbered excitedly about my "Mouseville Edition." Cousin Warren renamed it the "Flycrap News." They'd all laughed uproariously about my earnest publishing efforts. My stepmother laughed until tears ran down her face. The more they laughed the more hurt and angry I got inside. As usual, I didn't dare express my feelings; that would just mean I'd get a beating and then I'd be angrier than ever. So I simply simmered inside and thought, *I'll show them.* Looking back, I can see that my life was made up of a string of "I'll show thems." It was an attitude that was to get me through a lot in the future.

The next day John and Dolly found my enthusiasm contagious and said they wanted to help. I had chores every day: doing all the dishes from each meal, with Joy, making the beds,, ironing, baby-sitting a lot, and whatever else Stepmother said to do. As soon as my chores were done, we set to work on the paper. John folded papers, and Dolly printed "Mouseville Edition" at the top. When I'd finished ten copies with four painstakingly handwritten pages each, we got the old wagon out, put the papers in, and set off to claim our fortune. The paper was a bargain at five cents each, we assured each customer. We went down the road, stopping at each house, hawking our papers in newsboy fashion: "Get your red-hot papers now!"

Mrs. Harris gave us a nickel. The kids whose parents had the greyhounds said we were to come back later if we wanted money; their parents weren't home. Across the street we went to the poor lady with the headache. She still had a headache and said, "Please leave," so we did. Finally we saw the lady with the palomino out in her pasture. We hightailed it over there since she was hardly ever home. We explained the glories of our paper, and finally she asked, "Well, how much?"

"Just five cents."

"Hmm. What's in it?" she asked.

"Oh, the Cook's Corner with recipes, greyhound track scores, Hollywood tidbits ..."

She laughed, accepting the handed copy to take a look. "Hollywood," she mused. "Let's see what's going on there." She chuckled, playing us along. She looked, suddenly grew red, and said, "How many of these do you have?" We showed her all that were left, and she asked if there were any more back at the house.

"No, this is all."

She said, "Wait here. I'll get your money," and ran toward the house. She counted out enough money for *all* the papers!

"She sure must have liked them, to buy every one," I remarked on our way back home. Once there, we proudly announced our total success, counting our money in front of everyone and jingling the coins endlessly in our pockets.

It wasn't until much later that I realized that the palomino lady's initials were the same as the ones mentioned in my "Hollywood Tidbits," the news given to me by Mrs. Bannister from a few doors down. The lady with the headache also lived nearby. Her husband's initials were T. J., and we always thought that was a great coincidence. As a matter of fact, the other initials, C. D., were the same as the woman who raised the greyhounds, we realized at some point. The adults in my family discouraged me from making any more issues of the newspapers. I could never understand why—it showed initiative, kept us out of their hair, and made money, but they said they'd take the strap to me if I did that again. I think maybe L. K. spoke to them.

We never made another issue. Thus ended my budding career as a journalist or newspaper editor!

Chapter Twenty-Eight

ALLIES, FOR ONCE

One night in Tempe, when I was about twelve, I awoke to find that I was being molested. Usually I could run and somehow get away, but this time I woke up out of a dead sleep. At first I stiffened and tried to scream, but a hand was slapped over my mouth. "Shush, it's all right!"

I indicated okay with my eyes and face. The hand lifted cautiously. I waited a moment and then yelled loudly, "I want a drink of water!" and started climbing out of the bed I shared with my sister Joy.

I don't know what made me think of that; surely I was being protected by a father far more loving than the one I was facing with terror in my heart.

"Hush. I'll get you some water," my father said as he turned and went to the kitchen.

The minute the water faucet came on I made a run for it and locked myself in the bathroom. I had to go through my stepmother and Daddy's room to get to the bathroom, so I felt safe there. I didn't think he would come after me with stepmother sleeping right there in the next room; their bed was only about three feet from the bathroom door.

Actually, I probably didn't even think much about all that. I was just looking desperately for a place of safety. The main thing was that the bathroom door had a lock. I could keep him out if I went there.

A few minutes later I heard someone try to open the bathroom door. Then silence. Terrified, I stayed where I was, barely breathing.

Suddenly I heard another yell, not as close: "I want a drink of water." Then again, someone was trying to get in the bathroom door.

I stayed huddled in the corner in the dark silence, listening to water running in the kitchen. *Someone* was getting a glass of water.

Sometime later, after a long, long interval, I heard the rhythmical sound of my father's snoring, in the bed beside my stepmother. I was still terrified and afraid to even try to get out. I would have to go past him; what if he was really awake and only pretending to sleep? I couldn't pull that trick again! What could I do to protect myself if he was awake?

"Oh, God," I breathed, "please help me!"

Still I waited for what seemed like hours. Finally I released the lock and tiptoed out, past the sleeping, now benign, father. I crawled back into my bed and lay shivering and frightened, alone. I lay praying for daylight when he'd have to go to work.

Suddenly from the foot of the bed crept Joy, one year younger. Every sound carried in that little house. Our bed was right beside their room, about twelve feet away. We didn't dare even whisper. Joy said not a word. Neither did I. That day as soon as Joy and I were alone, however, she jumped on me.

"You think you're smart, running into the bathroom and locking me out, don't you?"

"What?" I'd stammered, hardly daring to believe what I was hearing.

I never dreamed that it had been Joy trying the bathroom door. When she couldn't get in there she'd run into Grandpa Bush's room and hidden under his bed, in the darkness. Grandpa never bothered us. All the while I'd thought I was the only one, there were two of us! It was the first I knew he was molesting her too.

That evening for no particular reason our stepmother said, "Slim, since when do you get up in the night to get those girls a drink of water? Let 'em get their own drink of water." He'd nodded and said he'd heard us crying in the night and went to see about us, because "they were having bad dreams."

Knowing now that there were two of us gave us courage. Joy and I plotted together to stop him. We talked about it all morning. Joy was positive that telling our stepmother was the thing to do. Gradually, I let her persuade me.

While we washed supper dishes that night, Joy and I called our stepmother into the kitchen to talk to us. Joy was just sure that if Stepmother knew it, she would stop it. I wasn't so sure, since she had said that about getting us a glass of cold water in the night. That sounded to me like maybe she knew what was going on but didn't want to interfere. But I went along with Joy, since she seemed so sure.

Somehow, being a year older, I was elected between the two of us to tell her. I took a deep breath and plunged right in. My great opening line was "Will you tell Daddy to stop bothering Joy and me?"

"What do you mean, bothering you?"

"He puts his hands on us, and we don't like it."

She said she'd take care of it. The next night at supper with everyone around the table she suddenly said, "Hugh, Jeanne and Joy want you to stop bothering them. They don't like it."

If she'd thought to startle him into some sort of compliance, she was badly mistaken.

He said, "Oh, they don't, huh?" That was all he said.

That's the last words he spoke to the two of us for over a year! When Christmas came the other kids had a few inexpensive toys, but Joy and I each had only one gift: a little rubber baby squeaky pig. We knew what they symbolized: squealers. That was all either of us got.

Merry Christmas.

Later that day, I queried Stepmother: "Who bought the Christmas gifts?"

"I did."

"Why did you get us those squeaky toys?"

"Because that's what your daddy told me to buy you. Next time you'll know enough to keep your mouth shut."

That's all there was to it. It was more than a year before Daddy ever spoke to us again.

When school reconvened after the Christmas holidays, I was standing on the playground at recess time. I huddled by the schoolyard fence in the cold, trying to stay away from everyone. All the kids were chattering about their gifts, telling what they got, boasting to one another. I only wanted to avoid anyone asking me, so I stood there by myself, shivering in the mild Arizona winter.

Suddenly, a strange teacher came over and asked me what I got for Christmas. Probably she saw me standing alone and wanted to make me feel better. When I told her I got a squeaky toy pig, she said, "What else?"

"Nothing," I mumbled.

"Well then, you must have been very bad," she stated as she walked off.

Yes, I thought to myself, *I guess it was very bad to try and tell on my daddy.*

Then one day at school, something wonderful happened, and briefly my world turned luminous and bright again. Our teacher told us that if anyone ever tried to bother us or to put their hands on us or make us feel uncomfortable, we could go to her. That afternoon when I got home from school I told Stepmother what the teacher had said. I said I had decided to tell the teacher if Daddy kept on bothering us. I was hoping that if I told the teacher it would stop Daddy. At last I thought I saw a way out.

"You just go ahead, Miss Smarty. If you do that your daddy will go to jail. Then Lee and Gil's father will come and take them away. I will take Dolly and John and go away. And you and Joy and Ray will be put into an orphanage. No, that's not right; you won't go into an orphanage because I will tell them you are very bad and they will put you in jail. That's where you will be spending your days! Now if you want that to happen to you and your brothers and sisters, you go right ahead."

After that I never hoped to be rescued by telling someone who could save me. Even a little kid knows when defeat has knocked on her soul and crawled into her very marrow.

The lesson that was being taught to me at home and at school was clear: you don't squeal on people. It does not matter if what they have done is right or wrong, just or unjust, kind or cruel. I was learning that life is not a matter of justice; it is a matter of being obedient to those in power and never, never telling on them.

Chapter Twenty-Nine

CLOAK OF INVISIBILITY

Child abuse, whether subtle or blatant, leaves the victim feeling totally helpless and hopeless. There is no escape. No way out. It's a small wonder abused children pick abusers for mates or become abusers themselves. Their sense of self-worth is about as large as a pimple on a bee's knee.

I learned a lot about lies my first seven years, and by the time I was eleven I had learned how to hide the truth of my family life from any outsider. As a youngster I had seen and experienced too much in my home; there was too much I could reveal, and I was a threat. I think Stepmother was constantly afraid that we would confide in someone about our home life!

I remember one time when they reluctantly let me stay with my aunt Nell for a week. I was twelve and was living in Bonifay, Florida. Aunt Nell's daughter Belle, who got her name from her two grandmothers, was my age and in the same grade at the Bonifay High School where I would enter my freshman year. I was thrilled to be going to a place where some others might play games with me, answer my questions, and let me work beside them. I was thrilled to be going on such an adventure for a whole week!

Aunt Nell was of medium height and just plump enough to be comfortable-looking and huggable. Secretly, I hoped she would want to hug me occasionally and maybe let me help her bake things in the kitchen, clean house together, go walking, and share thoughts. Such dreams sometimes made up my foolish childhood hopes but were never realized except for the year I spent with Grandma and Grandpa Love. Those were the happiest moments of my childhood, and although it lasted less than a year, it helped me get through the next two decades. It was the foundation for my dreams, like the hope-filled ones I was bringing to Aunt Nell's. At eleven, I was still young enough to hope.

Sunlight was stripping long shadows from tree branches and lacing them into the grass when we arrived at the house. My stepmother rang the bell, and the expectant minutes seemed like hours until Aunt Nell answered with what seemed a special smile for me. She even knelt down so we were on the same level as she told me how glad she was to see me. Then she and my stepmother began talking while I gazed hungrily around at all the lovely things. Suddenly I heard my stepmother's voice cutting into my consciousness.

"One thing I must tell you, Nell: Don't believe anything Jeanne tells you. She's a terrible liar."

Aunt Nell paused, and I thought I could feel her shrinking from me. I was just a skinny, ugly little liar, not to be trusted, not even to be listened to. How easy it is to be stripped of self-esteem! I was sure Aunt Nell would have nothing to do with me the whole week long, but she was a teacher and could think for herself. Instead she talked to me a lot. All week she questioned me and talked with me.

At the end of the week my stepmother came to get me. They were sitting in the kitchen at the old round oak table drinking iced tea when suddenly I heard Aunt Nell declare, "I want to tell you one thing, Jean. This girl is no liar!"

Stepmother's eyes skewered me and betrayed herself. I knew she was afraid, and I knew she would be dealing with me when we got home. I hadn't told Aunt Nell or anyone else a thing, but Stepmother would never believe me. Even being discreet seemed to get me in trouble. Like I said, there was no way out.

One time, before I learned the art of invisibility and that it was the safest way to avoid trouble, I let my rage spill over. I was outside, playing in the backyard. Nearby was an ant hill. I, who had up to that point always had a reverence for all living things, suddenly looked at that ant domicile as an inferior thing, a thing to be subdued.

I marched over to the ant hill with giant, angry strides and began kicking viciously at it. Busy worker ants ran in every direction as I destroyed their carefully and intricately constructed rooms. Why did I do it?

I didn't understand then, but later I realized that I was retaliating for all the helplessness and hopelessness in my life. Now *I* was the one in control. *I* was the one meting out unfair punishment with impunity.

You took away my homes and my family, I raged inwardly in a silent shouting monologue with my father. *You have beaten me and bothered me and forced me to your ways. Well I can do that too, and I will do it to these creatures who are as helpless against me as I am against you!*

Besides, I rationalized to myself, *Daddy puts poison on the ant hills to destroy them, so it must be all right for me to kill them, too.* How easy it is to learn the art of self-justification!

The rage quickly subsided, leaving me aghast at the chaos and destruction my feet had effected. Ants were running everywhere, trying to salvage what they could from their destroyed home. I immediately felt anguished that I had caused some other creatures to feel as I had been made to feel. The quality of being in control, of being able to be unjust and not fear retribution, the joy of power unlimited quickly dissipated. Had I wreaked all this havoc? Had I destroyed so wantonly? I was sick inside, and my little heart beat with anguished sobbing thumps.

It was the only time I remember breaking out in rebellion. I was not a fighter. I was a peace maker, and my style was to bend with the winds of change even when they were cruel and unjust. I got in less trouble that way. Eventually I learned to stay out of sight, walk softly, hang my head when forced to answer, avoid looking directly into eyes, and become as unnoticeable as possible. I became one of the "invisible ones." They make no impression and leave no aftertaste, and often you don't even realize they were there. If you were invisible, you were safe. And if you were a nonhuman in the first place, it was easy to be invisible.

What isn't human often goes unnoticed … by the self-centered. At the age of twelve, I was beginning to learn invisibility. It was my cloak of safety against the self-centered adults I lived with.

Chapter Thirty

MY THIRTEENTH SUMMER

I entered my teens the May after the "Mouseville News" was published, but I was not to have another summer with Gwen. The summer following the end of the eighth grade Daddy got another—well, it was more a bug than a bee in my opinion—bug in his bonnet thinking that the pot of gold had shifted back to his old hometown of Bonifay, Florida, while he wasn't looking. He moved us all back to Bonifay, into an old wooden house outside of town. First, though, we rented a house in the country from his relative, Lucille, for a short while. It was peaceful living in the country, and I liked living in this house with hills and valleys all around us.

We had a lot of my father's relatives in that small country town, and I came to love those aunts and uncles and cousins of mine. Having all that family to visit was glorious! Daddy's family was well respected in town. Most of them were big farmers, schoolteachers, or store owners. I quickly came to love my aunts and uncles and enjoyed visiting them. It made me feel like a Banty chick with a dozen Bantam hens clucking over me, just waiting to take me under their wings.

The high school where I began my freshman year was a big two-story brick building. It seemed enormous to me. As a new girl in a school where everyone seemed to know everyone else and to have grown up with them, and also because I was Aunt Nell's niece (she was one of the schoolteachers) and Belle's cousin, I acquired some instant celebrity status at school. Lucille was one of our aunts' sisters, and she also was a teacher at the high school. I had fallen into "family," and what a splendorous experience it was!

Cousin Belle was pretty and popular, a head majorette. She liked me to spend the night or weekends with her, and we seemed like good friends. But at school, even though we were same age and grade, she spent her free time with Cindy Well. I tried my best to be "cool-looking," like she and Cindy were. Occasionally Aunt Nell gave me Belle's outgrown clothes because I was still small and skinny, so I knew I was wearing the right things; however, in spite of all my efforts I never made the grade at school with Belle.

But I had other friends. In fact, I was elected treasurer of the class that year. Me, who hated and feared math! We all knew, however, that it wasn't a question of math skills but rather of popularity, and as new kid on the block I had instant status—at least at first. Eventually, of course, "new kid" wore off and I had to earn any status that was to be mine, but this time, at least, I was given a head start.

The day came when we had to give a speech in front of the entire English class. I was determined to do well. Lucille's home had a side yard with a large tree stump in the middle of it. I used to stand on it and loudly and boldly recite my speech. Over and over, I'd repeat it so that when class time came I'd be ready. I knew every word by heart, tongued each vowel perfectly, let the syllables roll out in ribbons of good enunciation. I practiced until I knew I could do no better.

A main country highway ran in front of the house. People from homes all around drove past our place, but of course I didn't know who any of them were. I did notice one man, however, because he always seemed to slow down when I was on the stump and drive slowly by, elbow sticking out from his open window.

Finally the day came to give my prepared speech. I got in front of the class, looked all around, and nearly fainted. My throat went dry, and I couldn't seem to breathe. My hands became so wet clasping and unclasping my notes that the sentences were no longer legible. I forgot everything I had memorized. My mind was a whiteout, a blizzard of unrelated words. For three weeks I'd practiced my speech daily after I'd written it up. For three weeks I had written and spoken the speech every day. Now I couldn't even think of the title. I broke out in a cold sweat and finally began to cry.

The high school in Bonifay was small enough that everyone knew everyone. Most of the teachers had come in to hear the speeches, which were being held after school. They sat there listening as my teacher asked me if I'd prepared for this speech. I could only stand and weep. Suddenly one of the tenth-grade teachers broke in and told him that every day he'd seen me standing on a stump in the yard practicing. What I hadn't known was that sound carried over the hills, and sometimes he'd pulled his car over out of sight and listened to how I was doing. The teacher told him it had been an "A" speech he'd been hearing, so on the basis of his word, I got an "A!" It took me a long time to overcome my "stage fright," but I did, by the grace of God. There have been other "stage frights" in my life, but I always remember how they can be conquered if you just work hard and do your best, especially if you have someone on the sidelines rooting for you. Approval and support are the two big growth hormones for human beings.

That summer, my father's sister asked me to come stay with them in Tallahassee because she and Uncle Bill were working all day and little Johnny was home alone. I'd been there a while when one day Aunt Cleo told me to walk Johnny to the barber shop. She asked me to go to the store while he was in there. She said Johnny knew the way by heart, which he did having always lived there; however, I didn't! Fear of being lost was a devil that had been riding on my back for years. Daddy and my stepmother used to tease me, saying they were going to move while I was in school. They never knew how unsure that made me, how vulnerable I felt. What would I do if they left and I was all alone in the world? Where would I go? Who would help me? I was filled with terror every time they mentioned it. I told Aunt Cleo that I didn't know the way. No matter; Johnny would lead us there and back. All I had to do was go to the store. She didn't know how frightened I was. I think the fear actually helped bring about the very thing I was afraid of. That is often true, I've noticed.

We got to the barber shop and Johnny went in. Somehow I found the grocery store, but coming out I couldn't remember which way to turn. My choice was random. After that, I walked up and down for a long time. Streets began to blend into look-alikes. I was caught behind bars of confusion, clawing frantically to get out. I knew I was completely lost, drowning in a sea of misdirection, strangled by seaweed of despair. Finally, I saw a policeman. Somehow I was able to tell him I was lost. "Where do you live, child?" his safe voice rumbled.

When I am frightened, I forget things temporarily. All I could remember was my real mother's name, address, and phone number. She too, lived in Tallahassee, and even though she had made no move yet to see me that summer, it was to her my heart fled when fear paralyzed my mind. Always, my heart yearned for Mother like an empty cup waiting to be filled. It was a cup destined to remain empty.

The policeman called her, and reluctantly she came to the police station to get me. She called Cleo and Uncle Bill. Little Johnny had been home and safe a couple of hours. He'd met a playmate, gone off with him, and forgotten about me being at the store. Seeing how my terror had abated the moment I saw her, something must have softened inside, and Mother said she'd like to have me visit her for a few days. Aunt Cleo said she'd be responsible for giving me permission. That was how I came to spend the summer of my thirteenth year at my mother's house.

Chapter Thirty-One

MY MOTHER'S HOUSE

My mother's house was cool, beautiful, and peaceful. The walls were pale blue like my mother's eyes. All the white French provincial furnishings were refined and elegant, and I was dazzled. It seemed as though she lived in a castle. My little half-sister Denise was four and a half by then. For a short time that summer I lived in a dream where I was a real part of my mother's life and my stepfather Harry and Denise were also my family.

Harry was always good to me. He'd been in the war, and his soul carried deep scars. He'd watched every one of the men in his platoon die. Only he lived, and he couldn't understand why. Some nights he'd wake up screaming and crying and sob for hours. On those nights, my heart felt like nails were being pounded into it, yet there was nothing I could do but lie there and pray for him. It would have shamed him deeply had he realized how his sobs carried through the rooms.

Before the war he'd been a very talented orchestra leader and a trumpet player. Did you know that trumpet players can lost their "lip"? It seemed that wartime had replaced Harry's trumpet lip with biting memories, stilling and killing all the music of his soul. It was an unfair exchange. By day he and a friend ran the burger and dog drive-in in Tallahassee. It carried hot dogs, burgers, fries, and shakes and was a very popular little place.

He made a good living, but his memories of the war haunted him. Eventually he turned to alcohol for tranquility and forgetfulness, but he was always gentlemanly in his consumption. Even when he was drinking he was nice to me.

One day he bought me a turquoise TV for my room. My mother made him take it back. She said he was "trying to buy my love." I don't think so. I think Mother might have been a bit jealous for Denise. Harry was just being kind and decent. I think he recognized my woundedness. Scarred hearts seem to have antennas that can zero in on another's pain. When he was drinking my mother was always after him, nagging and ragging, unable to see his haunting pain.

My mother was beautiful, intelligent, and self-sufficient. She was still working for the state as a secretary. She drove a yellow convertible and had gorgeous clothes. That summer, she bought me several blouses and shorts. I was so proud! My mother cared enough about me to buy me clothes! The clothes themselves weren't important; her interest in me clothed me in invisible robes of glory. Mother's sister Doris took me shopping and taught me how to pick out fabrics and coordinate colors. My summer was turning into a rainbow! Then Aunt Doris taught me how to sew a plain full skirt. My favorite was the white with watermelon print design. I made three skirts.

Grandma and Grandpa Love took me out to their farm for a few days. It was like heaven sitting in the deepening dusk with Grandma beside me on the porch swing and Grandpa in the rocking chair, listening to whippoorwills, crickets, and frogs in a symphony of the night. It was good to be hugged and introduced like somebody special and to know that I was loved. When my mother took me back home with her, Harry asked if I'd like to live with them. My rainbow had yielded a pot of gold! Breathlessly, I said I would.

The next day, they drove me to the old house in Bonifay and Mother told me to sit in the car while she talked to Daddy. She told him I'd decided I wanted to live with them. He said okay if that's what I wanted. I was free to go! With feet not quite touching the ground, I went in to pack my things. Little Dolly cried and hung onto me. I felt sorry, but more than anything, I wanted to go with my mother. I went out to my "secret room" to get my treasures. It was actually the old wood shed room built on the side of the house, but I called it mine and often sat out there to read. It kept me out of sight and safe. Now I wouldn't have to worry about being "safe."

It didn't take long to pack all my possessions. When I carried out my things and got in the car I was surprised to see how tired and worn-looking my Daddy was. I felt sorry for him too, but I wanted to go home with Mother. I wanted to have Grandma and Grandpa Love back in my life. I wanted their support and love. I wanted to be someone's daughter instead of a brat and a burden. I wanted to belong in a family. My heart was singing, but still I felt sorry too as we drove away to Tallahassee.

My mother's aunt had a daughter my age, Reba. That summer, Reba, my great aunt, and her husband Bill were going for two weeks to their cottage at Alligator Point. I was invited to go too! Life was marvelous. Reba and I frolicked and played on the beach up and down, every day. My aunt Estelle was handicapped, and each day Reba and Uncle Bill gave her physical therapy, moving arms and legs back and forth. She had muscular dystrophy. She seemed to expect life to minister to her because of her handicaps. Reba had to do all the housework as Uncle Bill worked in the city and drove down on the weekends. I helped Reba cook and clean.

On our last day at the cottage, Reba sweetly said, "Jeanne, you go on and enjoy yourself. This is my job, and I don't want you to help today. Go away and play so I won't feel guilty that you had to help work the whole time.

"I'd better help."

Reba smiled and said, "Get out of here!" Getting ready to scrub, she threw a big bucket of water and soap across the linoleum floor of the cottage and shooed me out.

So I left. I went along the beach picking up shells until suddenly I heard my aunt yelling for me. I came running back, eager to please her. As I approached, she began chewing me out: "What did you mean leaving Reba with all the work to do alone; the least you could do was help!" I tried to explain, but she kept yelling and beating my ears with nasty words, curses flying around my head. Being immobilized in a wheelchair didn't handicap her mouth. I hurried back to help. Had Reba set me up deliberately? I never knew. Maybe it's possible that she thought her mother would see her scrubbing the floor all by herself and praise her and thank her for all the help she'd been to her through the years. She didn't, but Reba got me back to help her, something I would have been glad to do in the first place.

Looking back, I remembered the first time I had been in Reba's house. There was a beautiful bowl of fruit on their dining room table. I didn't know Reba yet, but she was friendly and nice when we met. She invited me in and led me to the dining room.

"Here. Have a peach." She smiled, handing me one from the crystal bowl. I thanked her and took the beautiful-looking peach. I bit deeply into it as Reba began to chortle with glee. The fruit was wax. Just then her mother wheeled into the room and saw my tooth marks on the peach. She was displeased and made it very obvious. In fact, you would have had to have been deeply mentally challenged to have missed her displeasure! I was so humiliated and ashamed! Reba continued to laugh even harder when she saw she had gotten me in trouble. Now her mother was angry with me again. Was it really my fault? Had I misunderstood? Or had Reba set me up? I would never know, but I think I learned something about people and perfidy that day, Even though I still liked Reba, I never trusted her again.

Chapter Thirty-Two

<u>RETURN TO SENDER</u>

After I came back to my mother's house from being at the beach with Reba, I sensed a strangeness and tension in the air. Every time Mother saw a friend and had to introduce me as her daughter, there were lots of questions from surprised people. "Why Edna, I didn't know you had another child!"

Sometimes I innocently ruined it by telling them, "Oh yes, there are three of us!" without realizing that it was really embarrassing her. All those years she'd lived another life. She had social standing in the community and lived elegantly and graciously. Harry was from a well-to-do family, and he had married her not knowing she had any children. So I guess my sudden reappearance in her life was very hard. She began to look at me with a critical eye.

Soon she began correcting every word I said. "Your manners are atrocious!" she scolded. We can't learn what we don't know, and we can't know if we haven't been taught. I had never learned the things she wanted me to know. I tried desperately to learn from her and to please her, but until I knew better I reached across the table just as I'd always done when I lived with seven kids, Stepmother, Daddy, Granddad Bush, and cousin Warren at the table. With eleven hungry people all reaching for food, if I had waited for anyone to hand me something I'd have starved to death! No one said please or thank you, so I didn't know we should. I really just didn't know better. And of course I had never learned how to introduce anyone. The list was long: according to her, my clothes were awful and I said "ain't" and "gimme that"; in short, I was incorrigibly raw and unrefined. But I was willing to learn. I wanted to learn! I would have done anything to make her like me, to make her proud of me. It was not to be. Suddenly, it was as though she was on attack.

In addition, Denise had become terribly jealous of me being there. One night I was lying in bed on my stomach and Denise came into the room and climbed up beside me. Without warning she sank her little teeth deeply into my back. I screamed and tried to pull away so hard my back bled a little. My mother demanded to know what I was crying about. I covered for Denise and said "nothing," and little Denise said proudly, "I bit her." My mother spanked Denise because, as it turned out, the bite was really bad and I carried teeth marks for a couple of weeks.

Mother's fights with my stepfather over his drinking had escalated. It seemed as though they fought constantly. He booked a flight to Jacksonville on a plane for a glamorous trip for the two of them. I watched her at her makeup table as she got ready, black hair pulled back from a perfect face in a big chignon on the nape of her neck, brilliant ocean blue eyes intensified by her baby-blue dressing gown. She had the most elegant blue face powder. On her fair skin she was gorgeous when she wore it, but years later when I mentioned that blue powder to her she said they had taken it off the market as it had such a high lead content it was dangerous. Her manners were impeccable, like everything about her. She was always perfect, so perfect that everyone paled beside her. I loved her, I worshipped her, but I couldn't live with her. She didn't want me.

While they were gone, Denise and I stayed with Grandma and Grandpa Love. I loved being there, and I played with Denise and entertained her a lot. But inside I was beginning to miss Dolly and John terribly, because at least I felt wanted there. My own mother really didn't want me, Denise resented me, and Harry got into trouble whenever he befriended me. I only caused trouble there. I didn't belong. I would probably never belong anywhere, and why should I expect to? I was gross, ugly, dumb, unrefined. No matter which "home" I went to, it was made abundantly clear that I was deficient in all desirable things. But I knew that Dolly and John loved me. Theirs was the only love I could count on in the whole world, and I was longing to return to it.

When Mother and Daddy Harry came back, the fighting resumed. It was getting close to time for school to start, and I'd be going to a huge high school for my sophomore year. One day Mother announced that she was going to lay out all the rules. Chin jutting out, she laid down the law of expected behavior. I had to make good grades always. No dating before sixteen. I'd never even been out with a boy, but when I told her she just said if I ever gave her any trouble she'd call DYS to come and get me and lock me up until I was eighteen years old. I became as afraid of her as I was of my stepmother. Had I only traded an old hell for a new one?

The thought of the coming school year struck shafts of terror deep into my psyche. What if I failed? I hated math. I did okay in everything else, but I was no valedictorian. What if I failed math? Daily, she corrected everything about me. Sometimes I'd say something about Dolly or John and it angered her. She began to refer to them as "your precious Dolly and John" in a derogatory way. It's a funny thing: if you downgrade people you force someone to defend them. It became a battleground. Daddy Harry drank more, and I blamed myself, not knowing it had been going on for years. One night Mother and Harry were arguing loudly and I heard Denise crying. I sneaked into her room to comfort her. I sat there on her bed, holding her and hoping to make her feel better. That was the moment when she chose to tell me that I needed to leave; I was only causing trouble by being there and no one wanted me around. I could hear my friable heart shattering like icicles falling from roof to ground. The hard frozen ground of their shattering was only an echo of my heart's desolation.

I became very quiet the next few days. I was drained of every emotion. A raging torrent of thoughts went through my just-turned-fourteen-year-old mind. My stepfather noticed and gave my mother a hundred dollars and told her to go buy me a new coat for winter. I'd never had a new coat before in my whole life! It would have been wonderful. However, for whatever reason, my mother spent the money on herself and told him so. The fighting resumed, as he defended me. I no longer defended myself when Mother cut me down, but I appreciated his defense of me. However, it only caused more trouble in the end. There was no way out of what was becoming an ugly situation.

One Sunday afternoon I had been given ironing to do and I'd ironed all afternoon. When I'd finished all my work I knew my heart had made its decision. I said to her, "I need to talk with you."

"I know what's coming, but go ahead."

"I've decided it would be better if I went back to live with my father."

She told me that I was just like him with no manners and I'd ruined her life and she'd be glad to see me go back to my precious Dolly and John. Early in the summer after I'd gone to live with her, she'd received a hateful letter from Daddy saying that it was her turn to help raise her brats. Now it was his turn to take me back, she said.

Nowhere was where I really belonged, and no one was who really wanted me. Before I had always been able to believe that someday my mother would come for me. She would want me and I would live with her forever. Now I knew the truth. No one. Nowhere.

Mother called down to Bonifay to see where she should send me back—to Aunt Nell's or to Daddy's? That's when she learned that they had moved back to Arizona without even telling me or her! She got the address from my aunt, and to avoid "wasting money on a plane ticket," she bought me a one-way bus ticket to Mesa, Arizona. My aunt said that Daddy had gotten a job at the navy base in Arizona. Mother wrote a letter to Daddy telling him she was sending me back. Three days later I packed my clothes in a little suitcase and she took me to the bus station. Harry gave me money for food on the trip and for spending money. Mother told me how to budget it on the trip so I'd have enough for the three-day, three-night bus trip. Mother kissed me good-bye and told the bus driver to watch out for me, and the bus pulled away. She was already gone before it had finished pulling out of the station.

Chapter Thirty-Three

THE BUS RIDE

When the bus pulled away that night I was frightened. I could feel the darkness without creeping within until my mind felt smothered in black and my body was heavy and night-sad. Being told "Don't talk to strangers" when everyone was a stranger left me silent and alone. There was no moon hooking back the draperies of the night and no stars to help pin up the darkness. There was nothing but blackness, inside and out. I sat huddled in my seat, alternately freezing and burning up, trying to sleep.

After a sleepless night spent with my cheek laid against the window or sprawling across the whole seat when I could, I watched the darkness turn from coal black to ashy-dust colors. My ribs ached from the bar across the middle of the seat, designed to keep would-be snoozers awake, I supposed. The little purse I carried was crushed on one side where I had used it as a pillow against the window.

When daylight finally came I made my way to the bathroom. I meticulously combed my hair and washed my face, Mother's words echoing in my head: "Be a little lady." I was still trying to please her! I ordered like Mother said to, to conserve money, only I ordered even less because I wasn't hungry. When it was time to go, I climbed back on the bus and took my seat. I sat alone with my legs crossed at the ankles like Mother said ladies do. The miles unrolled in a patchwork quilt of town and farm buildings bordered with urban and rural countryside scenes.

I had become a people watcher as I grew up, so the bus held more interest for me than the scenery outside. I watched everything going on. One poor old man got on holding a little brown bag. Soon the bus began to stink with a rotten smell. He was a couple of seats in front of me, and I watched as his shoulders leaned forward. He seemed to be retching. His seat partner got up and moved, muttering, "He's eating limburger cheese!" The whole bus smelled like stinky feet. That was when I learned what limburger cheese was and how to identify it by smell.

Up the right side of the aisle about five seats from the front sat a young woman, maybe sixteen or seventeen years old, with ash-blonde hair and gray-blue eyes. She wasn't beautiful, but she was attractive. She sat alone. After a while a young sailor got on in his bell-bottom sailor suit with his sailor hat. He asked her if the seat next to her was taken, and she said no.

He put his long sausage-shaped duffel bag on the baggage rack above and sat and began to talk to her. At stops they ate together; then they'd come back on the bus, sit together, and talk some more. It was fun watching them and imagining how they might someday fall in love and get married. As day wore into evening, I saw him kiss her! He started French kissing her; at first she protested, but then she didn't. I didn't know what that meant, but I heard her say she didn't French kiss. I wondered how the French people kissed and how it was different from American kissing.

Some of the other passengers must have heard her too. They went to the bus driver and complained. The bus driver ordered them to stop disturbing the other passengers. The sailor boy stood up and whispered to her, "Let's go sit back here." I was sitting near the bathroom, a few seats from the back on the left. He got his duffel bag down and her makeup case and they strode down the aisle past me. He stowed the bags above their heads, and as darkness fell they resumed necking.

I had curled into a ball with my back to the window and my feet pointed toward the aisle so I could watch them from my empty seat. Finally, he stood up, pulled down his bag, and took out a blanket. It was white wool, with a navy stripe. I fell asleep with her sitting in his lap under the blanket. I didn't sleep well in that position, and I heard her begin to fight him.

"Be still; it will quit hurting in a minute."

The hours of the night rolled on, punctuated by sounds of breathing, groans, and panting. It was disturbing and frightening to me.

When morning came I heard him tell her they needed to freshen up. They took turns going into the little bathroom. She stayed in so long that the other passengers began to complain and pound on the door. When she finally came out her face was red and flushed and she was trembly. They whispered a lot, and she told him to promise to write. He said of course he'd write to her.

She asked him what if she missed, and he said, "Tell your mother."

"What?"

"Tell your mother you need help and she'll know what to do." Then he laughed. Whereas he'd been somewhat nice before, now he'd become cocky and sneering. Suddenly he stood up, grabbed his duffel bag, and said, "This is my stop. I've got to get off now."

He told the driver he had to get off, and as he did one of the passengers who'd complained yelled at him that he should be ashamed of himself. Her last words to him were "Please write me."

She sat red-faced and trembling, teary-eyed, staring straight ahead until her stop came to get off. The same old man told her as she got off, "Young woman, if you were my daughter I'd horsewhip you."

Beside the small-town bus station stood a nice-looking family, all grabbing her and hugging her, excited and glad to see her. She looked so bewildered, robbed of a precious gift she would have some day given to her husband by a man she'd never hear from again.

I had one more night to spend on the bus before we arrived in Mesa, but nothing that interesting occurred again. Rest rooms, bus stops, restaurants, cities, farms, and passengers began to blur until they all seemed like one huge ball of colored confusion and shifting impressions that threatened to roll over me.

Finally the third day arrived and it was my turn to get off. I had arrived!

The small drugstore where the bus stopped seemed almost empty. I looked about expectantly. No one seemed to be looking for me. I asked the time and learned that it was 2:00 in the afternoon. I had $4.21 left. Not enough for a taxi. I didn't know anyone. Since there were no familiar faces among the people outside the store I decided to go in.

Maybe they lost track of the time and are in there talking or reading a magazine, I hoped to myself, but no one looked familiar inside either.

No welcoming committee was there for me. I checked the phone book. There was no listing for them. In my hands I clutched the piece of paper with the address on it.

That crumpled little piece of paper was all I had in the world to connect me with anyone in this strange new city. The druggist told me that it was quite a little ways to the address I held in my hand. I said, "That's all right—just tell me the way."

He shrugged and asked, "Is no one expecting you?" and I replied that my mother had written a letter and mailed it a couple of days before I left. His face looked at my skinny little fourteen-year-old baby face with some consternation. He gave me directions, and I started out.

At first I was interested in the sights around me, my first impressions of my new home city. I kept walking. Soon I was looking only at street signs and at the sidewalk ahead of me. I walked a lot more. By now I only cared about putting one foot in front of the other. My eyes were mostly fastened on street signs and the sidewalk under my shoes as I continued to walk. Finally, I found the right street, and there was the house with the number right on it! I had arrived! At four in the afternoon I was finally home! Reenergized, I ran up the steps and knocked on the door. I could hardly wait to see Ray and Joy. The door opened slightly, and a strange lady answered.

"Yesss, a Mr. Jerry used to live here, but they've moved on."

Fatigue struck again, and I didn't think I could move another step. My throat was too raw and dry to even cry, but I could feel endless sobs welling up inside me.

"But you're lucky, dearie. I know where they moved to."

The lady's words broke through my consciousness, and a splinter of hope flared up against interior darkness. The lady knew where they lived, but they had no phone. She gave me directions to get there.

"If I had a car I'd drive you myself," she said generously.

Earnestly I replied, "Thank you, but I can't take rides from strangers."

I turned and once more began a walk that would last several more miles. As I finally neared the old stucco house where they had moved to, I saw Dolly and John and Joy playing in the yard. Weary beyond words, I called to them. Dolly heard and recognized me. She ran to meet me, and clinging to each other, we went into the house.

My stepmother glanced up from what she was doing.

"What are you doing here?" She was almost snarling.

"I-I c-came home," I said and explained that Mother and Harry had sent me back.

"Well-l-l-ll, I don't know if you can stay. We're full up; we moved into a house for seven, not eight people. I'll have to talk to Daddy and see," she said ungraciously.

Shortly after that Daddy walked in from work. "Jeanne's here," she blurted out without explanation.

"What is she doing here? I thought she wanted to live with her mommy!"

What ensued was not teasing, although that is what they would have called it. It was torture, designed to keep me uncertain about where I would be staying, how long my presence would be tolerated, whether they could afford me, feed me, or clothe me, and even if I was wanted there. This would go on for several weeks. In fact, it actually lasted for the rest of my three-year stay with them. They made jokes all the time about moving: "Go on to school, Jeanne, so we can move while you're gone."

As the sun abandoned the day and dusk dipped deeper into the twilight, Daddy drove me to the bus station to pick up my suitcase. The druggist told Daddy that he was getting ready to call the police to check on me and make sure I was all right and to see if I had found the address.

"Don't never need to worry about this 'un," Daddy muttered. "You couldn't lose her if you wanted to. I know," he added cruelly.

The next three weeks were a nightmare of uncertainty. My stepmother wouldn't tell me if I could stay or not, and thoughts tumbled through my head until my brain was a whitewater tumult of cascading fears and whitecaps of desperation. Finally, one day I burst out crying and said if I couldn't stay I'd have to find someplace to live, and I didn't know where to go.

"You poor dumbbell. You're here, aren't you?" she said scornfully. That was the way I learned that I would be allowed to stay—for now, at least. Nothing in my life was sure. Nothing was secure.

A few days later the letter from my mother came, telling Daddy that I was on my way, what bus I'd be arriving on, and the time. It had been sent back to the post office after the family moved and re-sent to their new address. It took over three weeks to arrive.

Their cruelty extended to anyone they could torment. For instance, when Mother's letter arrived they quickly sat down and wrote a letter to tell Edna that they had moved and to give their new address. In it they asked how I was doing. All my mother knew was that she had put me on a bus. Now, weeks later, they were writing as if I had never arrived there. I wonder if she was tormented? I never knew. She didn't call to see about me, and as far as I knew, she didn't even write.

My family always "joked" about waiting until "Jeanne is gone and then we'll move away with no forwarding address."

It was a joke that cracked the face of decency and slapped the smile of hope from my face. I never felt safe and was never secure again as long as I lived under their tissue-paper roof of broken dreams and torn hopes.

Perhaps that's how they wanted it.

Chapter Thirty-Four

MY LIFE WAS TOUCHED

I was not raised in church. No one in my Arizona family ever attended church, but when I was about six years old and in the first grade, a little girl asked me if I wanted to go to church and Sunday school with her. They came and picked me up. It happened to be around Easter, and the preacher kept talking about the Lamb of God. People were sobbing around me, and I kept punching the little girl and asking her why her mother was crying about a sheep.

I was very curious and probably loud! After church they took me home. The next day at school, I asked the little girl if I could go again with them, and she said if I wanted to go some more I could ride the Sunday school bus.

Eagerly, on Sunday mornings I would stand out by the road and wait for a church bus. Now I was only six years old and did not know my address or phone number because no one had ever worked with me. One Sunday morning when I got on the driver was different, but it didn't matter to me as long as I got to go to church. After I got back on the church bus for the ride home and the driver had delivered all the children, he discovered that I was still on the bus. I hadn't recognized anything familiar and so just kept riding. I didn't know my address or phone number, so the frantic driver had to retrace his entire route.

Two and a half hours later, I recognized my house. Everyone was out looking for me, and I was yanked off the bus while the driver explained that I didn't know my address or phone number. My father said that it would never happen again (and it didn't, because I was never allowed to go again). After that, each Sunday when the bus went by I could only watch with sorrowful eyes as they passed my house.

The first time when the driver stopped I told him that I could never go on the bus again. He said he was afraid of that. The Sunday school bus never came for me again.

At least that time I learned that they cared enough to look for me if I was missing. It was the first time I knew they cared that much!

A year or two later, a little girl in my second- or third-grade class wore a beautiful dangly gold-colored charm bracelet. She said it was "Rules to Live By." If we followed them we could never be bad and God would love us forever. Light swung off the ten figures. It was a promised land of golden hope. "Loved forever!"

All day long I nagged her to tell me the different rules and what they meant: "Thou shalt have no other gods before me." "Thou shalt not steal." "Thou shalt not commit adultery." (Something only adults did, so we kids needn't even worry about that one.) I learned them all from her that day. "Thou shalt not covet." "Honor your father and mother." But who was my father? A man I feared? My mother? Two women, neither of whom wanted me? Miraculously, a child with no Christian upbringing or background absorbed and retained all Ten Commandments, even without fully understanding them. There was just something about them that tugged at my heart and made the words somehow very special. They became my very own rules to live by.

The next time religion entered my life was when we were visiting our step-relatives, who invited us to church. Eagerly, I went along. In the Sunday school class the teacher asked who could tell her about David and Goliath. Several of the children raised their hands. I didn't raise my hand, but she looked right at me and asked my name. I told her and in my southern drawl reckoned as how I did not know Goliath, but David was in my stepbrother's class at school. All the children laughed, and the teacher turned an angry red. I was so embarrassed, but I didn't know why. I only knew that I never liked Sunday school again, although I still cared for church. I was already on the way to seeing myself as unacceptable, undesirable, and unwanted. Rejection had played a big part in my life and would continue to do so all through my school years. I had a long way to go and many more lessons in rejection to learn. This was only grade school! I was to become very sensitive to teasing, belittling, or being made fun of. I could not see the future and did not know that my present-day pain would someday become a gift of sensitivity and responsiveness for others.

When I was thirteen years old I was "saved" at a revival meeting I had been invited to. I attended a Southern Baptist church for awhile, but we moved so much that every Sunday I just went by myself to where I found a church I felt at home with. I have continued that practice through the years, seeking out that spirit of love. I learned early that it wasn't the denomination of church but was the spirit inside it that counted. Denomination doesn't matter; love does.

These were isolated events, forged across the years, but those links formed a necklace of love that "would not let me go." As my years lengthen, my certitude increases that God is a reality that touches each of our lives, yearning to let Him love us. There have been numerous interventions in my life that are unaccountable without a belief in a divine presence. How do I know God exists? I know, because I have experienced Him.

Chapter Thirty-Five

SAMUEL WHITMORE OF OBSCURITY, NORTH CAROLINA

The past three years had been the best of my life. We had come to Mesa when I was in the ninth grade, and I was now in my junior year. I had been there longer than anywhere I ever lived. I had a special group of friends all my own, I worked on the class yearbook and the newspaper, got good grades, and earned spending money from a part-time job in a local drugstore. The future lay before me like a precious gem, resting within the soft velvet box of a college degree. Yes, I would go to college! My dreams now had a possibility of becoming real. With my job, I had a way of making them come true. With the money I saved, I could work my way through to get that precious degree.

In addition, by carefully using some of my drugstore earnings I could buy clothes like the other girls wore. With normal clothes, makeup, and jewelry that conformed with the rest of the crowd, I was acceptable. By eleventh grade I was one of them.

I still worked hard at home, trying to make myself so necessary that they wouldn't send me away. That was an ever-present threat hanging over my head like the sword of Damocles, just waiting for any weak excuse to sever my body from my home, my self, from my family. Then I would have no one who wanted me and nowhere to go. What would I do if they kicked me out?

Of course, no one at school knew what my home situation was like or that my parents were constantly joking about "moving with no forwarding address and leaving Jeanne behind." At least they would say it was joking if we had visitors. In actuality, it was subtle and deliberate cruelty, as familiar to me as the shape of my hands or the color of my hair.

I worked in the drugstore nights and weekends and went to school all day. I was a jack-of-all-jobs at the little Rexall store: I worked the soda fountain and the grill, stocked supplies, and was the sales clerk. On weekdays we were open until 9:00 pm and Friday and Saturdays until 11:00 pm in case the doctors needed to call in prescriptions. I put in a lot of hours, because more than clothes or makeup, I wanted the money so I could go to college. I was saving most of what I made.

Outside of my year at Grandma and Grandpa's, this was the happiest time of my life to date, even though Daddy continued to try to bother me. When I was fifteen, my stepmother intervened one night when he was trying to get into my locked bedroom door. She told him he couldn't mess with me anymore. "She's too old for you to be whipping her like that. Besides, she could get pregnant."

"What about Joan?" he said. She hadn't moved out yet.

I heard her reply, "She's started her period too. Leave them alone." But he never did, totally.

I did not understand the implications of those words. The reader will have to draw her own conclusions as to whether the ashes of my innocence were entombed in a parental Judas coffin.

Finally Joy told my father that she was sick of her and her friends being pawed by him and went to live with a girlfriend. After she moved out I was alone in the bedroom. Most kids want a room of their own, but I was terrified. Daddy continued to try to molest me occasionally, even after that conversation with my stepmother.

In Mesa we lived about three miles from the small-town Main Street the drugstore was on. Each night after I cleaned up I walked home alone. It made for a long day! I went to high school full-time all day and then walked two miles home, changed my clothes, and walked three miles back to the drugstore. I was little and skinny and had waist-length hair. I guess I was pretty, but I was the original reserved "straight arrow." I didn't date because I'd been told that boys made up tales in the locker room about everyone they went out with. Even though I was so thin I was still full-busted, so I wore loose baggy sweaters and blouses and hunched my shoulders over so the boys wouldn't make choice remarks such as "Gee, I wish I had x-ray vision!" I lacked confidence for repartee and was too self-conscious to ignore their teasing/admiring comments. I was so shy that my nickname was Mouse, because I often walked so soundlessly that no one knew I was there. At home I knew that the less attention I called to myself, the safer I was. That's why I learned to walk quietly.

Strangely, I was popular with a group of really nice girls, girls who made good grades and were in activities like yearbook and school newspaper. I worked hard in school, and by working after school, besides what I saved for college, I could have money to buy my class ring or my prom dress or to do things with my friends, like an occasional movie on Sunday. None of my girlfriends were dating yet either. All together we were a really attractive-looking group, and people thought we had a clique. I never thought about it that way. To me, it was just the first group of girlfriends I had ever had.

One day my original girlfriend met a nice guy when she drove to the Air Force Base to deliver a load of meat to a restaurant for her parents, who owned a meat locker. Marilyn was a year older than me, as were the other girls. Anyway, Marilyn and Max had been dating for a while, and Janice and Ruby and Fern began seeing young air force men also. On Fridays the guys would all drive the forty miles from the base in Max's little car, rent one motel room together, and then drive back late, late Sunday night. Those nights the others would go to the movies or out to eat, but I never could because I had to work at the drugstore. Max told Marilyn one night that he knew someone named Samuel Whitmore from North Carolina whom he thought I should meet. A few weeks later they brought Sam and arranged for us to meet after I got out of work.

I knew right away that he was different. His mouth had a sweet, gentle half smile on it, and he was quiet, not loud or pushy like other boys. Samuel Whitmore turned out to be an Eagle Scout. He had been in the Scouts all the way through high school and was the original true gentleman. He really helped little old ladies across the street, and he took great pride in every job he did. In his air force uniform he was an extraordinary sight.

Handsome, tall, and tanned, he had curly, light brown hair and an endearing little brown birthmark on his cheek. I felt shy and awkward around him, but he had a gentleness of spirit that helped me overcome my shyness. We talked a lot that night. From then on, when I was available Sam and I were paired together on these twice-a-week visits. Then he began waiting outside the drugstore to walk me home. Saturdays by 10:00 pm I started cleaning up and the owner closed and locked up the pharmacy, and at eleven o'clock he would turn out the lights and we would leave until Monday.

Every Friday and Saturday Samuel was outside waiting to walk me all the way home. (I must have appealed to the Boy Scout in him.) Finally, after three weeks, he took my hand to hold. What bliss! That's really what it was: bliss! There's no other way to describe it.

He was always the gentleman; he talked without cussing or telling dirty jokes, and he didn't drink or smoke. Mac had chosen wisely for me. On Sundays I would go to the movies with the whole group, or sometimes we took a picnic to the park. After five months we were all playing at the park and having a picnic one evening, but Sam seemed to want to get me off by myself.

We left the group and were sitting on the blanket talking for a while when suddenly he leaned over toward me. I watched his blue eyes come closer and closer. His arms slid around my shoulders, his face met mine, and he kissed me. His lips were warm and gentle, and I knew that I had nothing to fear from this man. It was my first kiss. After that, we became inseparable. As time went on my thoughts were wrapped around him like a morning glory that was always in bloom. My life was truly glory! Our thoughts, our feelings, our very hearts seemed twined. Eventually Samuel said he wanted to marry me someday. We were not talking of right now, but later. I was a junior in high school and needed to graduate. He was still in training in the air force, but we both knew what we wanted and that we were destined to spend life together.

One thing I loved about Sam was his religious devotion. He was Southern Baptist and I—well, I was a Methodist, but only because that was the closest church that seemed to feed me. I went wherever I found the spirit of God. If Sam wanted me to become Baptist, I would. We both knew how important God was in our lives, so we didn't really discuss it a lot. We had no need; God was preeminent in our hearts and the way we lived.

Winter slowly turned its face away, and spring put hers forward. The prom was coming up. I told Sam and, half afraid of rejection, asked him if he would like to go. His face split with a huge grin as he promised to take me. "I thought you'd never ask!"

"I was afraid to. I was afraid you'd say no or be too busy or something." I was so used to rejection that acceptance of me or my ideas was a strange—almost frightening—concept. But I was thrilled! For a while every penny went toward buying a beautiful prom gown so he would be proud of me at the ball. After weeks of saving and miles of walking, looking at prom dresses, I finally brought a beautiful pink gown, my first formal. It was made of pink clouds, cotton candy, dreams, and starlight sparkles. It was the most beautiful prom dress that ever had been made. It was for Sam.

That weekend when Sam came I told him all about the gown and how beautiful it was. I had given up weeks of college money to buy it and was so pleased. I thought he would be too, but he was very silent all through the evening. I knew something was wrong. Before he went back that weekend he gently told me that he had called his parents and talked to them during the week. He told them about me. They said that as a Christian and Southern Baptist he couldn't go to a dance. I was a Methodist and enjoyed dancing. To Sam's parents, dancing was sinful, so he was not allowed to go. Sadly he said I should go with someone else.

I should have known better than to believe in something so beautiful! Desolate, I put the dress away without even trying to get a refund. I put it at the back of my closet, living in superstitious fear that the dance was a portent and that soon I would have to begin putting my dreams, my hopes, and my love away. I grew afraid. Things were different now. Our times together seemed dragged down with unspoken, unrealized sorrows. I felt smothered in sadness at times. The Damocles sword was back, hanging heavier than ever over my head. Surely God would not take this away from me! I wanted only to belong to Sam, to be his forever, to do his ironing and bear his children and cook his meals. I wanted my life to be with him for always. We both loved God; surely a loving God would not destroy the one great, lasting happiness I had ever known! But as our time together unfolded I began to understand that in some way, Samuel seemed as afraid of and as controlled by his parents as I was by mine! My heart was filled with foreboding.

Prom night arrived. All my friends were chattering excitedly, planning parties at one another's houses, talking about their dresses. When I came in, the talk would stutter to a self-conscious stop. I knew that they pitied me, and I hated their pity.

Although Sam had said to go with someone else, I couldn't. Without him it would have been rusted tin in my mouth and scorpions in my heart. Marilyn and Max and Janet and Gene and the others went and had a ball. For them it was their senior prom. Sam didn't come down that weekend, and for the first time in many months I walked home from work alone. Silently, I went to bed feeling very lonesome. My brittled heart found it hard to breathe. It was like it always had been before Sam. Loneliness was a slimy, descending slope I couldn't help slipping down. The silence had little bugs in it, creepy crawly bugs with stingers, designed to torment and terrify. That weekend they crawled all over me, stinging constantly.

The next day was Sunday. On Sunday mornings I would get up and walk to the little Methodist church in town, a little farther than the drugstore. On Sundays Sam stayed at the base and went to base chapel in the mornings and would come down late, about 3:00 pm, with the guys. I was not raised in church as he was, but I had always felt pulled toward God and had found Him on my own at age thirteen. As usual, I went alone to church that day with a heart full of aching questions. I didn't even know if I would see Sam that day. Yet somehow I knew that this was hurting him as much as it was me. We'd work things out, I promised myself. After all, we loved each other, our love was good, and God was in it. I went home feeling a little better. Sam didn't come that Sunday, but after the prom week was over, he was once again waiting to walk me home. He said that he had to honor his parents' wishes because that was how he was raised. He said that his father had said that a man's good name was worth more than great riches. Well, I loved Sam and Sam loved me, so we put the prom behind us and went on, walking in ignorance toward a pit deeper than any I'd known.

The day came when Sam was entitled to leave-time. He made plans to go home for a month and visit his family. He was going to tell them all about me and our plans to marry after I graduated from high school. Sam was nineteen then. We had forged our plans carefully so no one could say we were being impetuous or too hasty. I was a ball of nerves, wondering how his parents would respond, especially after their attitude about the prom. I waited impatiently to hear from him. He had promised to write every day. When I knew he would have arrived in North Carolina, I rushed home each day to read the eagerly awaited letters he'd promised to send. Meantime, I was writing him, of course.

Three weeks went by with no word from Sam. Was my stepmother destroying them? He *said* he would write, and Sam was a man of his word. Yet, not a single letter came. Why? Why?? Why??? Finally one day there was a letter from North Carolina. But it wasn't from Sam. It was from his mother and father. Not your typical "Dear John" letter, this one said, "After much prayerful and deliberate consideration we have decided that you are not the right life partner for our son. Our son has been raised in a Southern Baptist church all his life. Also, as the son of the plant manager he has a certain social position to uphold. Our son Sammi was allowed to go into the military to fulfill his tour of duty and to give him time to mature. Sammi will need to complete college before he will be ready to support a wife. Sammi agrees with us that you both need to see other people and get on with your lives. We will be praying for you. Sincerely, Mr. and Mrs. Whitmore."

My heart was broken, but each day I had to go on to work and to school. There was no one I could talk to. All the agony and grief had to be bottled up inside me as I talked with the girls, helped customers, and tried to act normal at home. When I got home I would get my school clothes ready for the next day, skip most meals, and just go to bed. That was when I learned what solace hard work could be. At school I worked even harder. At night I practically ran home from school and changed and ran to work. At work, I stocked and cleaned frantically between customers, hoping to ease the pain in my heart. At night, I ran all the way home, hoping my heart would burst inside me and I'd not have to see another day. Finally, the month's leave Sam had was over and he returned to his duty station at the air base. I knew he was back; however, weeks went by and I did not hear from him. Finally one day Max delivered a letter from him. It was the "Dear John" letter, asking me to see other people and he would also, as he had decided that was the right thing to do.

On the Sunday after that I was sitting on my bed crying great racking sobs I'd held inside for weeks. By then I had given the family the barest outline of what had happened since they all knew something was wrong. I lay there, crying and rocking back and forth on my bed. Across from me sat my sister, a silent witness to my grief. She never said a word but just sat, as if by her being there she could help carry my pain. The bigger the heart becomes to contain the joy of living, the greater the grief it can hold to contain the pain of leaving.

After a while, listening to my muffled sobs, my stepmother came in and said, "You know, you really need to give his parents a piece of your mind for causing all of this trouble." In her hands she held pen and paper. "Write to them; it will make you feel better to get it off your chest. Here." She thrust paper at me. "I'll even help you write it. After you're done you will feel better, and then we'll just get rid of the letter and forget it."

With that she sat on the side of my bed and told me to begin writing. She dictated the words to me, telling me word for word what to write. She even made some jeering jokes in the letter. At the letter's end she told me to say that if Sam ever wanted to get married again they'd better let him as he "would probably have to." I was so naïve I did not know what that meant. There had never been a sexual relationship between us, because we both wanted to save that for marriage. We had made the decision together to wait.

Although they were vitriolic words that I never would have written on my own, their very caustic nature helped alleviate some of my pain temporarily, at least. Then after it was all written, she took the letter, saying she would get rid of it for me. "Now then, don't you feel a little better already?" I was numb from grief and also stunned at this first-ever sign of sympathy from her. I hungered for her sympathy, for her love. Could it be possible it was no longer being withheld?

With her arm outstretched, she offered, "Hand it to me now, girl, and I will take care of it for you."

It seemed harmless enough to give it to her since she promised it would be destroyed. I gave it to her with a little queasy feeling in the pit of my stomach, and Stepmother carried the letter out to "get rid of it" for me. I thought she meant she would throw it away or burn it up or put it away. A few days later I asked her what she had done with it.

I was beginning to feel remorse for being angry with them and writing the things she told me to write. I asked God to forgive me. I decided that if she still had it, I wanted the letter to throw it away myself.

That was when she told me. "Sorry, dearie, but I've already mailed it to his parents!" I couldn't believe she would do that! That's why she had insisted I include his address at the top of the first page! She meant to do this all along!

"They deserved it," she sneered. Perhaps I wanted to believe that she had done it out of unexpected sympathy for me. Perhaps I simply couldn't accept another monstrous betrayal in my life at that time. At any rate, I chose to believe that she had done it because she cared about me. It was only much later when I realized that it was her Machiavellian sadism at work again. By sending it she was guaranteeing that Sam and I would never get together again.

It had been an angry, ugly letter, and I was struck with remorse thinking of them receiving it. I cried and prayed and asked God to forgive me for mean thoughts. Finally I sat down, wrote a letter of apology, told them what had really happened, and asked them to forgive me.

I received a letter back from his parents, telling me that the fact that I wrote such a letter and then blamed it on my stepmother confirmed their feeling that I was not the right person for their Sammi. Furthermore I "had not been raised in any church regularly and was now attending a Methodist church." That seemed to be totally unacceptable to them. They promised to pray for me and told me again to see other boys. One day when she was snooping, my stepmother found the letter and was angry that I had apologized. I no longer had the spirit to even discuss it.

Later, Max said that Sam was having a hard time and his dad had come from North Carolina to Arizona to spend some time with him. Max would not tell me any more. Later I learned that Sam's father spent two weeks with him in a motel. Sam was on the verge of a nervous breakdown. I always felt so worthless, like maybe I wasn't good enough for someone like him. I drove myself harder and harder. Nothing helped for a very long time, but at least hard work got me through it without doing something desperate. Sam wasn't the only one having a hard time; we just approached the problem from different angles. I worked and refused to think of it; he dwelt on it, worried, and wept.

I never saw or heard from Sam until years later, after I married Joe and had two little boys. A minister started up a little Southern Baptist missionary church near us. I usually had to walk to the church since Joe always wanted the car so he could go to a bar. Maybe he'd come home in the wee hours of the night; maybe he wouldn't come at all—I never knew. I had walked to the little Southern Baptist church nearby with the boys. We had been going for a few weeks when one Sunday morning, there was Sam in the pew across from me! After the service he said hello, and I left. There had been an older woman with him. I didn't try to evaluate my feelings; that part of my life was over, and I had two children and a marriage that was a living hell to deal with. I put Sam out of my mind. I'd often see him after that. Sometimes the woman about ten years older than him would sit beside him.

I encountered her one day, weeks later, when I was at the grocery store with my little boys. After we had chatted about nothing for a few minutes, she came directly to the point.

"Could you stop by my place on your way home for a few minutes?" Her eyes seemed to plead. "It would give us a chance to visit, and there's something I need to ask you." I didn't know why she wanted to see me; certainly I didn't especially want to see her, but reluctantly I agreed to go.

"I can't stay long; I've got so much to do." Her eyes lit up a little and she gave me directions. In a few minutes I had gathered the boys and walked to her street where we searched for the apartment.

Her apartment was simple and sparse, as was she. She wore no makeup, and as I had surmised, she was ten years older than Sam. She was a nurse, she said, and as I sat on a chair in her apartment she was packing nurse's books into orange crates. She asked me questions all about Sam, like how long I had known him, how we met, had we gone together, etc. I told her that we had been engaged. She asked me for how long and what had happened. I told her of our plans and about the letter from Sam's parents. All this time she was packing books into orange crates and moving things around. I told her that the letter from Sam's parents had really been very nice and they had said they were going to pray for me. Her reaction was one of soft cynicism and sorrow. She was sad and very nice.

Later I ran into her again and we talked about Sam. She told me they had been engaged but when she saw him saying hello to me each week, she asked him who I was and asked if he had ever been involved with me. He replied that there had never been anyone else but her in his whole life! My Sam, who had been so upright and honest! She said if he would lie about that he would lie about anything. I told her I was sorry to hear that because Sam was a wonderful man and (again trying a little self-hypnosis) that his parents had been real nice in the letter. She said sarcastically, "I bet!"

Then she told me something that stunned me. She said she'd been watching me with my little boys and talking about me with others. She learned that everyone felt I was a really nice person! She said that if I couldn't please Sam's parents, then neither could she. She said that she believed in telling one another absolutely everything when you got married. She confessed that when she was in college she had gotten real wild. After she'd gotten saved and started going to church, God had forgiven her.

She then told me, "God forgives, but people don't." She was thinking of Sam's parents, I surmised.

I always thought that maybe Sam did not really lie to her; maybe I just was never important enough to mention. After all, she was a nurse, and so smart. I was nothing. If I hadn't known it before, I certainly did after marrying Joe!

Poor Sam. I hope that you were able to fulfill your parents' dream of the perfect wife, social position, 2.5 children, and the little garden you intended to plant behind the house, just like your dad's. But above all, I hope you had wonderful sturdy sons who became Eagle Scouts and a beautiful daughter whose laughter fills your heart with joy. I wish you a job that you are fulfilled in, and at the end of the day I pray that your heart still skips a beat when you see your life partner. And I wish you grandchildren, so that you can learn unconditional love. That was my prayer for Sam. I didn't know how to pray for myself.

Chapter Thirty-Six

LESSONS LEARNED

For all these years I could see how God could love everyone else, but not me. I knew everything about me. The adults in my life had told me about myself: every bad word, every nasty thought, every unworthy deed.

I could not forget my sins nor forgive myself. I had been taught to think of myself as a monster, when actually I was a shy, frightened, inexperienced child, innocent of any egregious acts. Evil deeds indeed! What damage we can do to trusting little minds that believe what they are told because it is an adult saying it.

Verbal abuse is greater than we realize. When a parent belittles a child or mate, embarrasses him in front of others, ridicules or denigrates him, he is reduced in esteem and ego. Eventually all self-respect dies. That's when truancy, delinquency, and trouble all begin. It is the first step on a pitted road leading to the great dismal swamp. How many well-intentioned parents are already unwittingly walking that path now? There is only quicksand at the bottom.

It wasn't until I had grandchildren that I realized what God's love was really like. We are His children, and whether we are being "naughty or nice," He still loves us, just as we still desperately love our children and grandchildren regardless of whether they've been bad or good. Love—unconditional love—is not based on what we do but on who we are and whose we are. We may be disappointed in what our grandchildren are doing, but we don't love them less. The same of course is true of our children, but somehow for me it became even clearer with the grandchildren. God's love is like a bullet of sunshine that can shoot through any cloud, regardless of the heaviest gray steel it is made of. And it can strike anyone of us, regardless of how many coats of Kevlar we wear.

God's bullet of love—that was what struck me when I was seventeen and met Sam. It pierced my heart with dead-eye aim. The subsequent mistakes I made that led to me abandoning college, giving up hope, and marrying Joe are another story for another time. My heart was crushed; my life was over. Nothing could equal this slimy morass of hell I was living in. "Nothing ever again can be this bad," my seventeen-year-old mind told me with certainty. I thought I had been *raised* in hell, but now I knew hell really was life without Sam. It turned out that I didn't have the faintest notion what hell truly was until I met and married Joe.

But even in the pits of hell, where our feet stand mired in clay and our heads are wrapped in a darkness that permeates heart and soul, there can come piercing love: sun-shots of revelation and hope. Perhaps it is only when we are hurting that we are open enough to learn. I only know that the intervening years, with the death of two of my beloved three sons, the years of torment with Joe, and finally marriage to a decent, kind man who adopted my three sons and gave me two wonderful daughters who grew to maturity with my one surviving son, were years of learning for me.

I obtained training and became a medical assistant. Today I am a phlebotomist and the current president of our county's Association of Medical Assistants. I found hidden talents that I did not know I had. Today I am an artist with sculptures, paintings, and photography frequently on display. I have won awards for some of my artwork, including a national one. I take college classes. Today I am a respected community member who feels loved by many. Today I no longer believe I am stupid. Today I have self-respect and take pride in my work. Today I am the grandmother of five precious grandchildren who have benefited from the knowledge I gained from those long years of pain.

Recently I worked on a ballerina I was sculpting, but for all my pains it wouldn't come out right. The sculpture was fine, just like God's original creations are. But the finishes I applied, coat after coat, bronze, pink, and black antique, just didn't blend right. My art professor approached, looked at it, listened to my discontent and dismay, and replied, "Jeanne, your sculpture is good. It is the steps you went through that you are unhappy with. This is clay, not bronze. You tried to make it look like something it wasn't. Let's cover it with floor wax, buff it up good, and dust it with clay dust from the incinerator." When we did, it looked great! I was so pleased.

"You would never have gotten this finish, though, if you hadn't gone through all the things you did. Look at all the stages you had to go through in order to get you where you are." He was still talking of the sculpture. I was thinking of life.

I have more to give because of what I suffered. I am more of a compassionate, caring human being because of the stages I went through. There are many ways of looking at suffering. It can embitter or isolate one. Or it can enlarge and free one. The way we accept pain has much to do with the way we are shaped by it. The pain that imprisoned me for most of my childhood years and many of my adult years has become the very agent that freed me. But I had to let it go. I had to be willing to learn from it. I had to be willing to grow—and growth is not always easy or pain-free. When the seed within cracks the casing of shell, pain is experienced. But so is growth.

Certainly I am scarred. Certainly my perceptions are super sensitive at times. Certainly I am self-demeaning, timid, afraid to stand up for myself, too quick to believe that others find me stupid or of no value. My problems are not all solved. But I am more whole than I ever dreamed I could be. If it was hate that tried to destroy me and pain that plumbed the very depths of my being, it was love that delivered me. Love for myself. Love from others. Love for others.

Now the time has come to share that pain, that story with you, in the hopes that any seeds of destruction and weeds of abuse may be pulled up before they sprout. It is nearly impossible to change the abuser unless he wants to be changed. That is not my job; I am not capable of that sort of therapy. But for the abuser, there is hope. The desire to change and the remorse at what you are doing and the lives you are warping is the first step.

There are agencies you may contact that will help you and allow you to remain anonymous. But there are other abusers out there, and I especially write this for them. They are the unknown abusers. They are unknown to themselves. They do not recognize themselves as abusers.

They are those who demean, who put down, who ridicule, who shout at, who intimidate, who use sarcasm, who embarrass, who belittle, who insist on control. Think of your mate, your children, your class, your patient, the people you are in charge of, those you arrest or pass judgment on. How do you relate to them while they are in your life? Think of the position in life you hold. Is it one of authority? Is so, how do you handle that authority? How do you administer it? All parents have authority over their newborn children. As they grow and develop their own personalities, do you insist on absolute obedience, absolute control? Do you treat as you were treated or as you wish you had been treated? Or are you in a position of having to accept authority in the job, on the site, in the classroom, in the hospital or jail? How do you react to it? Do you then go out and treat others as you have been treated? Or do you touch their lives with the understanding, gentleness, and justice you yearned for?

It is for the unaware abuser that I especially write. You are in danger of unwittingly ruining lives, scarring little (or big) souls, and destroying the lives most precious to you. Do not let yourself go any longer. If you think you might be an emotional abuser, do something about it now! Contact your nearest Abusers Anonymous, read and learn what you can from your library, see a therapist or a priest or psychologist, or contact social agencies or a school counselor or medical associations to see where help is available—do not delay. The life you save may be the one you cherish most.

If you are the abused, tell someone in authority now. There is help and hope for you. Don't be a victim any longer.

I am a survivor!

If you expected my childhood story to make sense, know that dysfunctionality knows no limits or bounds.

It has taken me eighteen years to record these events.

Only now can I grieve for the child who was.

Every child is raised by a different set of parents. My story is not my sister's story, nor my brother's. I only know that the Lord has given me the ability to remember and recall for a reason. As well as having to forgive my tormentors, I have the desire to give the message to other abused children that there is hope.

Life doesn't have to be full of sorrow and pain. No one deserves to undergo such treatment.

Children raised in a dysfunctional environment have no life skills to make wise choices as to what constitutes a good future mate. Many times they are driven by an overwhelming need to escape their tormentors. It's easy for someone to be a charming, charismatic, person when all is going well. Observe them when the car breaks down, the toilet stops up, or the puppy chews up their best shoes.

If you have escaped the abuse, the choice is yours now. What you choose now can affect the rest of your life. Pick wisely.

I'm including a list of traits of abusers. Choose wisely. Dung or divinity. God bless.

ABUSIVE TRAITS

1. Pushes for quick involvement
2. Jealous, excessively possessive
3. Controlling
4. Unrealistic expectations
5. Isolates you from family and friends
6. Blames others for problems or mistakes
7. Makes others responsible for his or her feelings
8. Hypersensitivity
9. Cruelty to animals or children
10. Playful use of force during sex
11. Verbally abusive; also possibly causes sleep deprivation
12. Rigid gender roles
13. Sudden mood swings
14. Past battering but claims that abused made them do it
15. Threats of violence; if they say it they think it
16. Drug or alcohol abuse that grows worse over time

Run, do not walk, away. *You* deserve better, and your *children* deserve better.

<u>HOW TO REPORT CHILD ABUSE / NEGLECT: 1-800-962-2873</u>

Victim

- Name
- Date of birth
- Name of daycare/school and grade
- Current location/address/directions/phone number
- Allegation(s) of maltreatment(s)
- Other siblings in the home
- Race/sex
- Social security number (SSN)
- Location
- Home address/directions/phone number
- Relationship to alleged perpetrator

Alleged Perpetrator

- Name
- Race/sex
- Date of birth
- Location
- Work address/phone number/directions
- Home address/phone number/directions

Reporter

- Name
- Address
- Relationship to victim

Other Important Questions

- What happened? (physical/behavioral indicators)
- Where did it occur?
- When did it occur?
- Why did it happen?
- Who did it? Who is the allege perpetrator?
- How did it occur? (Example: If physical abuse, did the alleged perpetrator use an instrument or their hand to hit the child?)
- Is there potential danger for the protective investigator in approaching the alleged perpetrator or the home?

Dedicated to my little brother, Ray.

**Life became too painful to continue living,
and he recently ended his life.**